Jen

Management Musings from an

"Accidental Sabbatical"

Thoughts of work, life, home ... and dogs

Jennifer Hansen

Jennifer Hansen

ISBN:1541171551
ISBN-13: 978-1541171558

Jennifer Hansen

**DEDICATED TO:**

My Mother and My Father
My first teachers.

Iz, Lilo, Lani … and Dolly
You each said so much—without ever uttering a word.

And to David …
Who helped me find my way.

Jennifer Hansen

Author's note:

Grammatical, punctuation and style elements—not following
typical literary practices—were used intentionally for effect.

# INTRODUCTION

It was never my intention to take a "sabbatical." I always thought that was something professors did, or highly intellectual folks who were lucky enough to work for companies that funded such an endeavor, or just people who placed little value on having a steady income.

Since the time I was fifteen years old—I worked. In fact, I can't remember a time when I didn't have a job. As a child, I worked weekends in my dad's warehouse packing orders of nuts and bolts. In high school, I worked retail at the mall—sometimes working seven days a week. And during college, I worked full time and went to school full time—and still managed to graduate in 2 ½ years  (yes, it can be done).

For the next 20+ years I worked steadily—and successfully. I have been fortunate in my career thus far. I was promoted many times, received awards and was honored by groups and associations. I worked for one of the most revered companies in the world—The Walt Disney Company. I led a business and a large team of people to accomplish some pretty amazing things.

I worked hard—and a lot. I traveled across our country meeting interesting people. I spent more time on a plane than in a car. Long days, business dinners, and working in hotel rooms at night were the norm. But I loved it.

I had a boss once tell me your job should truly be "FUN" 80% of the time. 20% is the stuff you don't like to do—hiring, firing, reports—whatever it is you don't enjoy. But the rest, that 80%—should truly be fun. And when that ratio shifts, when the "Fun" side of the teeter-totter begins to drop—well that generally means it's time to change.

In the past few years, my journey has led me in some new directions. I decided to go back to school and get my MBA at MIT Sloan School of Management. This was a life-changing experience. And other than marrying my husband—it's the second best decision of my life!

And I decided to resign from my position at The Walt Disney Company. My time at Disney was wonderful, rewarding, inspiring, at times magical and also—life changing in many ways. Our division was undergoing a reorganization and with it, my role was changing. I knew in my heart it was time. It was time for me to do something different—to do something more. And if I was going to leave, now would be the right time for the company and for me. Much like school, we learn, we grow and we graduate. It was time for me to "graduate" from Disney.

My entire life, I lived by a list. Whether at home or at work, I mapped out my plan and I made it happen. For the first time in my professional career, I didn't have a plan—and I took a leap.

I thought I would resign and jump into another position at another company. But the universe had other plans for me.

Through my time at MIT, I ended up working on a multinational project, in a completely new industry that literally took me all over the world. Having left my fulltime job, I was able to devote 100% of my time to the project and did some pretty important work.

And personally, well … the universe had some plans for me there too. About six months after I left Disney, my mother was diagnosed with cancer. In the past several years, I missed many family events because of my schedule. And now, when my mom and my family needed me the most, I was here. And I am happy to say, my family and I walked the road to recovery with my mom, and today she is doing great.

When I quit my job, my health wasn't good. I was overweight and suffered from typical stress-induced ailments. I never exercised—who had time when you work 14 hours a day?

So, I began walking. I walked everyday outside and began to see things I had never taken the time to see before—like lightening bugs and butterflies. I lost weight, felt great and found a new energy for life. My husband and I even took up several new hobbies together—our favorite—shooting sporting clays!

My husband and I never had "human children," instead we had "canine children." We raised Newfoundland dogs and added a little hound too—they are our kids. Over the years, we did everything with them. We showed them in conformation dog shows, we competed with them in obedience and water rescue training—we even traveled with them. Some may say "they are just dogs"—but I know differently.

In the past year, two of our Newfoundlands became very sick

requiring a lot of care. During this time, I was here with them—to help them, to nurse them, to love them … and to learn from them. The many precious moments I had with "my kids" during this time were a true gift.

My husband has a favorite expression: "You are where you are supposed to be, doing what you are supposed to be doing."

No, I never meant to take a sabbatical. But that is exactly what I did.

I believe now my *"Accidental Sabbatical"* was not so *accidental*. Over and over, I witnessed events and people coming into my life at the exact right moment:

- A windfall of money arriving just when we need it.
- Time to be with family during an illness.
- A long lost sorority sister reaching out just when I needed uplifting.
- Casual contacts turning into professional opportunities.
- Missed years erased by sharing constant moments with my dogs in their final days.
- Old high school acquaintances becoming sources of inspiration.
- A new hobby bringing new friends and a new way of life.
- An instructor teaching me more about myself than the sport.
- A negotiation stretching me and reinforcing my path.

No, there was nothing "accidental" about this time in my life.

This book is a collection of musings. "A-Ha" type moments I experienced during my *"Accidental Sabbatical."* I have compiled them here in the order in which I wrote them.

I thought about eliminating some of these passages. But I left them in—all of them. Because how the chapters unfold is also part of the story.

Some of these pages were written during light-hearted times of joy. Others during periods of frustration and yes, even fear. But each represents a lesson. A lesson for work. A lesson for home. A lesson for Life.

I share with you my thoughts. My discoveries. My journey. I hope you enjoy this collection. And in reading this book— perhaps even experience your own "A-Ha" moments.

I used to think we were two selves: our "professional self" and our "personal self."

I now know—that is not true.

There is just ... self.

My true self.

My best self.

And I give myself to you ...

Jennifer Hansen

# Caterpillar ...

Jennifer Hansen

7.17.14

# Be Fearless

What is *Fearless?*

Yes, fearless means brave, courageous, determined. But think about it differently.

I think Fearless means to Move. When not sure of the future—we push through anyway. And in doing so—that *Forward Action*— that *Fearless Step*, gives us the power and the strength to do more and more and more.

True fear comes when we stop and sit too long. That's when uncertainty sets in, when wonder and worry lead to fear.

But when we take Action. When we Move.

When we Decide. When we Deliver.

In every step—we are Fearless.

8.18.14

# What's in the Mirror?

**Take the mirror test.**

We are faced with hundreds of moments filled with decisions, choices, annoyances and joys ... Everyday life.

Take this test:

Ask yourself—in 10 years when you look in the mirror—what will you think of this moment?

Will this really **matter**? If not—let it go ...

Will you know you **gave it your all**? Keep moving forward ...

Will you be **proud of your decisions**? Choose wisely today ...

Will you know you **made a difference**? Always serve others ...

In 10 years who will you be?

**Someone shaped by your actions today ... so ACT!**

9.19.14

# Eyes Forward ... Way Forward

When I was first learning to drive, I remember something my instructor told me. I was easily distracted by the things right alongside me—the car next to me, the guardrail that was close by—and my car would swerve all over and I felt nervous.

My instructor said, "keep your eyes forward, way forward—focus on where you want to go—way out in the distance. Your peripheral vision will take care of the things close by, but by focusing on the distance, your brain naturally follows your eyes and the car will steady."

He was right. Almost instantly, as if the car knew what I wanted, my hands steadied, the car straightened and I was driving along in my own lane—exactly where I wanted to be and heading in the right direction.

Business (and life) is a lot like this. We can easily be distracted by the things right in front of us, or bumping into us. But by keeping our "Eyes Forward ... Way Forward," we stay steady, heading in the right direction and arrive exactly where we meant to go!

10.1.14

# It's Like Breathing

Have you ever been asked, *"What do you do for a living?"* That's easy to answer.

And have you ever been asked *"What do you like most to do in your job?"* Still pretty easy.

But how about—*"What are you really good at?"* Now not so easy.

Think about Breathing ...

Your whole life depends on it—and yet you never give it a thought.

In our careers, there are moments that feel effortless.

Moments that come so naturally, they are almost automatic.

That is what I call the **"Professional Breath."**

It's as basic as breathing and as complex as oxygen pumping through our veins.

This is our professional spirit.

We all have one.

Finding it in ourselves, and fostering it in others, is key to serving as a leader.

10.27.14

# Momentum ... through Balance

Balance is more than a "buzz word." There is a natural order that strives for balance.

I didn't particularly like physics in school, but Newton's Third Law stuck with me: *"For every action, there is an equal and opposite reaction."* This isn't just true in physics, chemistry or other sciences. This is true for everything—in business and in life.

This is about balance.

When we worry, eventually fear overtakes us and we are stuck, not able to move forward ... No movement.

When we constantly operate at full throttle, eventually we burn out, and we stall ... Again, no movement.

In both cases, we can't seem to get momentum. Any extreme will eventually cause an even more extreme and opposite result.

But by striving for balance in our thoughts, our communication and in our actions, that's where we find true positive momentum for ourselves and our teams!

12.11.14

# A Step

Whether it is a tree growing from an acorn; or the first step of a marathon, all "success" started with one small action.

When climbing a mountain, is the victory really reaching the top? Or maybe the real success is in the precision of our steps and the choices that we make along the way. After all, anyone can land by helicopter on the top of a mountain—but is that the same kind of "success?"

True success is not just achieving BIG things.

Sometimes, it's about starting small things.

Don't let the size of the task at hand scare you.

Seize the small moments and ACT!

Greatness will soon follow!

1.12.15

# The Leader Behind the Curtain

As a little girl, I was mesmerized with "The Wizard of Oz." The Land of Oz, its vibrant colors and dazzling characters, was a magical place. And just like Dorothy, I believed "the Great and Powerful Oz" was the man making it all happen.

But as we see in the film, there was no great wizard. There was simply a man ... a man "behind the curtain," who helped everyone believe that the Land of Oz truly was a special place. The magic didn't come from the wizard at all—it was created by each of the individual characters all believing in that magic.

I think leadership is a lot like that "wizard." It's not about being all knowing and "great and powerful." Rather, it's about instilling a _belief_ in what's possible. It's about **creating a vision** for the future. It's about **building a framework** that allows everyone to **thrive and succeed.**

_Being a leader is a lot like being "the man behind the curtain."_

Thousands of years ago, the great Chinese Philosopher Lao Tzu wrote these words—a timeless reminder for leaders:

*"A leader is best when people barely know he exists, when his work is done, his aim fulfilled, they will say: we did it ourselves."*—Lao Tzu

1.19.15

# What's Your Language?

Do you find watching weather forecasts amusing? There are days that are forecasted as "Partly Sunny," and other days as "Partly Cloudy" ...

Aren't these really the same thing?

I suspect there is some meteorological difference between the two, but in either case we will see a little sun with some clouds, or some clouds with a little sun.

But how do you feel when you hear the two forecasts?

If you live in the North where many winter days are grey, hearing "Partly Sunny" can make you think, "Ahh! It's going to be a nice day." And hearing "Partly Cloudy"—well that just feels like another grey day.

As leaders, and as people, our words have tremendous impact on others. Just the simple word choice we use in a phone call or in an email can have enormous impact on how our message is received. Two words may be defined the same way, but the effect they have may be worlds apart.

Communication is not about words, it's about conveying an intended message.

Choose your words to match your message.

Partly Sunny is always a better forecast!

1.19.15

# How Leaders Fight Human Nature

As human beings—we resist change. Often we order the same item on the menu at a favorite restaurant, arrange our furniture the same way, and drive the same route to and from work. *Habits are comfortable ... and change is not.*

But as leaders, we embrace change. We challenge our teams to think differently, we develop new strategies for growth and we create a vision for the future—often one that is different from today.

As leaders, we have learned to fight our own human nature and instead focus on the benefits of change. But a leader's willingness to change is not enough. It takes the whole organization understanding <u>the need</u> to change in order to embrace it and move in new directions.

When a team is rowing a boat, if only one person is paddling, the boat moves in circles. *It takes everyone paddling in the same direction to reach a new shore.*

Businesses thrive and grow <u>because</u> of change. When was the last time a "comfortable habit" led to amazing success?

2.18.15

# Manage for Today—Lead for Tomorrow

There is a lot of discussion about the difference between "managing" and "leading." There are books, blogs, posts and even conferences dedicated to this subject. There is a thought that this is an "either/or" scenario—one is either a Manager or a Leader. But to truly impact business, I believe you need to do and be both! It is just a question of timing.

**"Managing" is about tactics.** It focuses on what needs to be done today, right now and in the present. **"Leading" is about vision.** It focuses on where the business is going, in the near future and the distant future.

Think about driving a car. You first decide where you are going, the best route to take and when you plan to arrive—**that's Vision—and that's Leading.**

But the maneuvers you take along the way, how you actually steer the car, how fast or slow you drive, what lane you choose—those are **Tactics—and that's Managing.**

**A car needs both ... and so does Business!**

2.26.15

# Expert or Apprentice?

As a society, I think we perceive great leaders as experts in their field. And yes, there is truth to that. Most leaders have great accomplishments to their names, thus we think of them as "Experts." But is being an "expert" what makes one a great leader?

Think of Albert Einstein. His discoveries changed the world. But it was the pursuit of the unknown, the study in new directions that were his greatest contributions. He could have continued to write about one topic the rest of his life—a topic he was an "expert" in—but would that have had the same impact on society? Of course not.

The impact of a leader does not come when he or she is operating as an "expert," only focusing on the areas that are known and comfortable. No one is remembered as a great business leader for doing more of the same. We don't say "he was a great leader because he maintained the status quo."

The impact for the organization happens when <u>you</u> get out of the "comfort zone" and continue to challenge yourself to learn new things, embrace new technologies and keep your eyes on the changing horizon.

The gift of a leader to the organization and to the people around him/her is to lead as an "Apprentice"—always learning, asking questions and guiding the team in new directions for the future.

I choose to be an Apprentice ... Always!

3.3.15

# Leadership—An Art or a Science?

As young professionals, we often perceive that business leaders have some sort of secret knowledge—a sixth sense about which products will sell, where to invest, which countries to expand into, how to finance a particular deal ... And many successful business leaders do all of these things. *This is the science of leadership.*

But is science enough? You can have the most innovative ideas in the world, but it takes something more.

It takes the ability to lead people. An understanding of how to build a team and the sensitivities of how to motivate an individual. It's knowing how to create a blueprint that maximizes the strengths of individual players— who when brought together—form a team that brings the "science" to life. *This is the art of leadership.*

Is Leadership a Science? Is Leadership an Art?

Yes!

3.30.15

# To Lead—From the Front, the Back or the Side?

As a society, we perceive leaders in front. They are often the "face" of the organization—and we assume they are the "brain" of the organization too.

But a true leader understands the importance of shifting positions. There are moments in which it's important to lead "from the front"—when it's time to set the strategy and vision. This is leading with the <u>entire organization</u> in mind.

There are times when it's important to lead from behind, knowing how to incent and motivate a team. And in the face of victory, allowing the group to shine and celebrate its own accomplishments. This is leading with <u>the team</u> in mind.

But the best leaders pivot to a third and critical position—to lead from the Side. This is being a partner, a guide, a mentor for those working with you and for you. It is knowing when to encourage, and knowing when to step back. It's knowing when you need to step in and knowing when to let others take the reins. Leading from the Side is not about the organization or the team. <u>It's about the individual.</u>

The science is leading from all sides.

The art is knowing when!

4.13.15

# Leader—Know Thyself

All great (and even not-so-great) companies and organizations have a leader at the top—from large global firms, to national businesses, to local non-profits. Each has the responsibility to establish the vision, make decisions, provide direction and manage people.

But is each leader the same?

If the job and responsibilities were relatively similar, wouldn't the qualities and characteristics of each leader be equally similar? Of course not ...

What makes a good leader? Being able to meet the expectations of the job.

**But what makes an Exceptional Leader?**

It's knowing the kind of leader you are. It's knowing your personal strengths, and the areas of "un-strengths." It's knowing where you personally add value and knowing areas where others are needed. It's also knowing your team. It's knowing where the strengths are on the bench and knowing where you may need to build in order to achieve balance.

One person does not make an organization. It is a combination of talent, skill, effort and experience. An Exceptional Leader does not know everything about everything at an organization. Instead, an Exceptional Leader knows everything about himself and what is needed to achieve success for the organization.

This weekend, I had the pleasure of experiencing the Boston Symphony Orchestra conducted by Andris Nelsons. This was the first time I had the privilege of hearing this world-renowned orchestra. About halfway through Strauss, I realized that I was watching and focusing on the various musicians—I was rarely watching the conductor. And yet, it was under his direction that the music was not just being played, it was magically coming alive.

Clearly, Andris could not play every instrument himself. He needed to build a team, with each musician complimenting those around him. One area could not overshadow another—if we only heard the violins and never heard the percussion—well that would affect the overall performance. He needed to build the right team, with the right musicians—each complimenting one another. He created Balance.

An Exceptional Leader ... sees success.

An Exceptional Leader ... inspires the organization.

An Exceptional Leader ... builds the team.

An Exceptional Leader ... seeks balance.

An Exceptional Leader ... Knows Thyself!

4.28.15

# Timing is Never Wrong

I am always amazed at stories of people missing tragic events. I remember after 9/11, a gentleman late to work dropping off his child at school, arrived just as the first plane flew into the World Trade Center.

Or a former professor of mine, in Nepal at the base camp of Mt. Everest, left the trip a few days early due to illness—and was gone mere hours before an avalanche descended.

In my own life, one morning driving to work, a car sped through a stop sign inches in front of me. If I had been just a few seconds earlier—well, I wouldn't be here today.

As professionals, we do everything we can to get the desired results. We hire the right people, we associate with the right colleagues, we pursue the right opportunities ... we attempt to put ourselves in the right place—at the right time.

In every leader's career, there are moments where deals fade and opportunities pass; and there are moments where deals are won and businesses flourish.

The only difference in these moments—Timing!

I have never been a very patient person. And I like to be in control of as much as possible. But I have learned that there is one thing I can never control—Timing.

Professionally and personally, I have learned that everything that is meant to happen will happen—*Exactly at the Right Time!*

5.5.15

# What Makes a Winning Team?

As business leaders, we often need to assemble a team. And of course each of us strives for a "Winning Team."

But does it just happen instantly?

Is it a skill?

Is it luck?

For many, the focus of building the team is on the players. And yes, that is a VERY important element of any team. Ask many coaches in sports and he or she will tell you, it all starts with the players. But what is the right mix of players? Do you want all "legends"—those with years of successful experience? Or do you want a "rookie" team—inexperienced but confident and willing to go to the moon and back?

Most good coaches will tell you that the mix of players has a lot to do with the coach. Some coaches excel at working with experienced players—they understand how to refine and motivate to keep the "legends" focused and winning. Other coaches excel at developing "rookies." They understand how to bottle the energy and focus it on a specific goal.

You can't start to build a team until you know your own strengths. And you can't build a balanced team with all "legends" or "rookies"—you need a mix of both.

Some people stop there, but there is one more important element in building a team. What type of culture does this team represent? This is not about the logo or the mission statement of the company. It's about the heart and soul of the organization. It's about what makes the team tick and ultimately succeed.

Many years ago, I managed a team that I would describe as "cut-throat." They were a mix of "legends" and "rookies," they were driven and competitive. All good things you may want on a team. But the culture, inspired and fostered by their former manager, was one of fear and lacked trust. This team should have been winning—they were certainly the right players. But their culture was bringing them down; they couldn't succeed no matter how hard they tried. For me, recognizing this was important, but fixing it changed the game!

Some people believe that you can't change culture. While others believe culture just happens naturally. I think this is partly true. Culture can be changed! But it takes the leader recognizing it and deciding the type of culture that is needed—for this team of players to succeed.

Knowing who you are as a leader is the first step in building a winning team. Carefully selecting the players to create a balanced team is the next step. But then determining the environment in which they play—the culture that you want to foster—that is the "secret sauce" in building a team.

It is this trifecta that makes a group of individuals not just a team … but a WINNING TEAM!

5.12.15

# The "Means" or the "Ends?"

Many of us are very goal oriented. It's not just about meeting expectations—but exceeding them. We set sales goals, production goals, time to market goals, expansion goals, profitability goals ... Success is gauged on meeting the goal. The more we exceed expectations, the more successful we feel.

I am just as guilty of this. As a student, it was about the grade on the test or the report card. As a young sales person, it was about how I did against last year. How much over goal did I finish? And when I was balancing grad school and a career, it was about hitting deadlines.

Today, as a business leader, I believe the true "win" isn't just about reaching, or exceeding the goal. Yes—that is important—and absolutely necessary (and still thrilling)!

But winning has two parts to it.

The first is achieving the goal. But—equally important—is what did I learn along the way?

By focusing ONLY on the "ends," we might just miss valuable

lessons during the "means."

Think back to the last strategic plan or report you produced. The objective was to produce a meaningful, professional report. And I am sure you did. But do you remember the steps you took along the way to produce the plan? During that process, what did you learn about the company or about yourself? Did it help you evaluate your business differently? Did you discover a new way of looking at the business that will help you in the future?

It's easy to recognize the nuggets of learning when we fail. We quickly analyze where we went wrong and try not to repeat that step. But what about when we achieve the goal? There is learning to be had then too. There is always a nugget of learning—if we look for it.

As a business leader, it is a necessity to focus the organization on the "Ends."

But it is also important to place value and celebrate the "Means."

**The lessons we learn on the path to the goal may actually be the true success.**

5.26.15

# It's Not the Words ... It's the Energy!

Have you ever been in the presence of someone, in a meeting or at a party, and you thought, "Wow, I'd like to spend more time with this person?"

Picture a conference room. The room is filled with people at all levels within the organization. The senior leader comes into the room. He's walking very fast, head slightly down, he doesn't speak, he doesn't make eye contact with anyone—he's lost in his own thoughts. He's carrying a notepad; papers are falling out of the pad. He seems to be perspiring a little. He sits at the head of the table, he noisily spreads his papers—he apologizes for being late and then talking very fast says "John, let's get started ..."

How do you feel right now?

Even just reading this, I bet you feel slightly anxious. And how do you think the people around the table feel? The pace is high, the stress level even higher. Do you think they have confidence in this leader—are they annoyed or worse still—do they fear him?

Now picture the same conference room and the same people around the table. Everyone is talking. The senior leader walks into the room quietly, he walks up to an individual, shakes his hand, putting his other hand on the man's shoulder, looks him in the eye and asks about his kids. He greets another individual, as he walks evenly with his head up, to get a cup of coffee. He then sits at the middle of the table. He takes out a small notepad, his movement is even and his demeanor is pleasant, yet confident. He looks around the table, smiles and says "John, let's get started ..."

Now, how do you feel? You almost want to know what happens next in the story don't you? You like his style, you feel comfortable, you trust this will be a productive meeting and you have confidence in this leader.

What is the difference in the two scenarios? The words used to start each meeting are exactly the same. So what is different?

## The difference is ENERGY!

As leaders, we spend a lot of time focused on WHAT to say. The exact words, the exact timing ... but leadership is not about words. It starts within ourselves, a quiet confidence in our own unique abilities. A confidence that no matter what the situation— we will handle it appropriately.

Being a leader isn't about what you say or even what you do. Your energy is understood long before your words are even heard.

**Leaders let their energy do the talking for them. What's**

it saying for you?

6.2.15

# Are You Adaptable?

Many executives define themselves by a specific industry or title. And for some, that is easy—"I am a Doctor ... a Lawyer ... an Engineer ..."—all very reasonable descriptions for some.

And others relate to a specific industry—"I am in Healthcare ... in Automotive ... in Advertising ..."—again for some, this defines their profession.

But did you ever stop to think what really defines you?

It's not what we ARE—rather it's what we DO!

Many of the great CEOs of our time have moved from industry to industry—from Automotive to Entertainment; from Tech to Government; from Healthcare to Finance ...

What one skill unites each of them? They are ADAPTABLE!

It's not the industry or function that defines these great CEOs. It's their ability to quickly asses their surroundings, establish a vision, develop a strategy ... and once again ... To DO!

We must constantly challenge ourselves to learn. There are lessons to be gained from other industries and other people. The key is recognizing that lesson—and doing something with it!

The key is being Adaptable!

6.15.15

# Are You Driven?

We say a strong professional is DRIVEN. But what is really the force behind the drive? Some professionals are *Driven to Succeed*—while others are actually *Driven to Avoid Failure.*

The word "Driven" makes you think of a car. We drive a car to reach a destination. Sure we try to avoid potholes, speed traps and accidents along the way. We do these things to stay safe. But these aren't the ultimate goals of driving—we are driving to get somewhere, a chosen destination.

There were times early in my career, when I was driven to avoid failure. At all costs, I would not lose and I would not fail. Today, I understand the importance of failure. Failure is not the opposite of success. Rather, it's the lessons we learn along the way to ensure we reach our destination.

As leaders, it is up to each of us to help others drive—not to avoid failure—but to drive towards success. There may be a pothole or two, some we may hit, others we learn to avoid, all while focused on the road to success.

As a Leader, I am Driven to Succeed!  How about you?

6.23.15

# Now

We often live in the future. We anticipate market trends, future customer reactions and competitive disruptions. We <u>must</u> keep our eyes on the future in order to prepare our business.

But if we ONLY focus on the future we lose sight of the present. We can become so blinded by our future plans that we might miss important milestones or trends happening today. Traffic counts for the business are higher than ever before. A customer wrote a letter celebrating an employee. Sales of a new product surpassed our highest forecast. A new employee just landed a big new client ... These are all important victories to acknowledge ... *Today!*

And is our brand as relevant today as it was yesterday? Are today's customers getting the attention they need? Are our employees better today than yesterday? These are all important, and possibly troubling trends, that may need our attention ... *Today!*

Celebrating milestones today ensures there are more milestones to celebrate in the future.

And addressing important trends affecting the business today stops the snowball before it becomes an avalanche.

As leaders we must lead for the future.

As leaders we must lead for today!

6.26.15

# Change Your View, Change Your Perspective!

Today, I did my most hated outdoor chore—weeding the patio. We have a large cobblestone patio, and those pesky weeds grow in between practically every stone. In years past, I started at the bottom of the patio and worked my way up. And with each weed I pulled, all I could see in front of me was a sea of more and more weeds—it felt like I would never get it all done. It was a discouraging task and I must confess, by the time I reached the top of the patio, my weeding performance would be rated "sub-par."

Today, I did something different. For no good reason, I started at the top of the patio with my back to the rest of the weeds. I could see only the weeds I was actually working on and the clean weed-free patio in front of me that I had just completed. The entire time, in front of me, I could only see all I had accomplished.

Yes, I knew the remaining weeds were still there behind me—but instead of feeling discouraged, I felt encouraged! It's funny ... I got that patio weeded faster than I ever have before. And I was determined to do a great job—when I finished there was not one stray weed left on that patio.

So what was different? In both cases, I had the exact same size job to do—a job I really dislike. But I changed my perspective—I literally changed my view, and it directly impacted the outcome and my own performance.

As leaders, we set the goals for the team. But after that, where is the focus? Is the team looking at the work left to do? Are they focused on the weeds?  Or can they see all they have accomplished?

**We create the vision—but it's important to create the right view too!**

7.6.15

# Is Your Air Stale?

Look around your organization. What do you see? I bet you see talented, smart, dedicated people with a proven track record in the industry.

Now think about Innovation! When was the last time the team created something new? Not just a tweak—but Revolutionary? When was the last time the company instigated a disruption?

Companies begin with a SPARK! A spark that smolders into something that really shakes things up. But over time, companies shift—the focus becomes execution, maintenance, day-to-day management. And as new people are hired, they are hired from competitors, from within industry—people who think and act just like the rest of the team. We start to believe that the industry or business is so unique, so different, that only people who have done the exact same thing could possibly succeed.

**And everyone starts to breathe the same air.**

But what created the SPARK in the beginning? How did innovation really occur?

It was a group of people coming together, with different experiences, different backgrounds, differing thought. And that combination—led to a SPARK!

Sometimes our air starts to get a little stale. It's up to us to test the air—and breathe new life into the routine.

**It's up to us to always be looking for the next SPARK!**

7.14.15

# Lead Business with Your Head ... But People with Your Heart!

Years ago we were taught, "there's no emotion in business; good leaders are tough leaders."

Early in my career, I believed these same things. I thought if I was to be viewed as a "true professional," I had to leave my emotions at home.

But years later, I know this is wrong.

Business decisions should be made with our heads. But when it comes to people—well that's where we need to lead with our heart.

As human beings, we all want to be successful in some way. We like to hear "good job" and to feel a sense of accomplishment. But as human beings we also make mistakes. Our environment (either at work or at home), our prior experience, and even our specific skills and talents, affect our performance everyday.

When a staff member makes a mistake, we want to ensure that

mistake does not happen again in the future. And as leaders, we have two options in how to handle the situation.

The first option—reprimanding the employee to make sure the mistake is clearly recognized as what it is—a terrible mistake. It is assumed with this knowledge, the employee will automatically not repeat the mistake.

The second option is to create a teachable moment. But a teachable moment isn't just for the employee—it's for us to learn too. We both must understand why the mistake happened to begin with and, more importantly, how to handle the situation differently in the future.

As a leader would you rather have an employee who can identify what is wrong—or someone **who knows what right looks like**?

The other day I overheard a woman complaining about her puppy. Whenever he has an accident in the house, she takes a newspaper to him—but he still keeps having accidents. My husband and I have spent years training dogs. So I was not surprised when I heard this—of course the puppy is still having accidents. She had focused on what was wrong, but forgot the most important step—to show the puppy what is right!

People are a lot like that puppy. We all make mistakes—we don't want to—but we do. But after awhile, being hit with a newspaper over and over just makes a really unhappy puppy—and a really unhappy employee.

Businesses are made up of human beings all working together for a common purpose. As the leader, our job is to ensure success for that business. But in order to do that, we must ensure success of the people within that business first.

How do we do that?

Through understanding. Through service. Through accountability. Through compassion. Through patience. Through teaching. Through inspiration.

Through Leading from the Heart!

7.21.15

# Rain—It's a Matter of Perspective

The other day, I was taking my morning walk. It was a hot and humid morning. I was about 10 minutes in and it started to rain. It was a light rain, so I kept going. I was on a new trail that day; it felt great to be outside—and I really wanted to finish my walk.

It started to rain harder, the sky grew darker—but I kept walking. At one point, I paused and waited under a tree. I thought about a friend of mine—I could actually hear her voice in my head saying "you should turn back, it's raining." As if rain alone was dangerous. I knew at this point, she would give in and turn around. But I decided to wait.

The rain lightened up, I kept walking and soon it stopped altogether. It was suddenly a lot cooler, there was a light breeze, the sky was beautiful and I was seeing new things on this beautiful new trail.

How many of us have colleagues, friends, even family members that when things go off course, when the unexpected happens, they whisper in our ear, "it can't be done. It's time to quit." How many of us set out on a new path and suddenly find ourselves "walking in the rain?"

Some people will always assume that "the rain" is an obstacle and something to avoid. But just like on that hot and steamy morning, the rain actually cooled me off and allowed me to keep walking.

Who's to say that "the rain" isn't a blessing? It might just be a lesson in disguise—we've just got to ride it out.

After all, rainbows only appear after a storm!

7.26.15

# Just Be ... Just Do!

Scroll through any social media newsfeed and you will see post after post of people trying to tell you tricks, gimmicks, and techniques of all the things you should do to win, to get rich, to be happy, to succeed ...

We are often accused of being a society and a generation that wants a "quick fix." And these posts and countless sites for advice are further proof.

Is it really that complicated? Do we really need another "9 sure-fire ways to be a better leader?"

I only know of one.

**Just Be ... Just Do!**

*"Be"* is knowing who you are. Knowing what's important to you, what you will accept—and what you won't. Years ago, we thought there was one set of rules in our home life and a different set in our professional life. Now we know that's not the case—one set of rules for both. Who you are, the values you respect, what and who you choose to surround yourself with, all of that is the same

all of the time—that's who you are.

*"Do"*—Now act on it. Treat others based on what you value. Speak from your heart. Move towards the goal you imagine—always! And inspire those around you.

It's really that simple.

No gimmicks …

No techniques …

No lists …

**Just BE! … Just DO!**

7.31.15

# Be All Heart ...

What does it mean to be **All Heart**? It means how you live your life, the way you make decisions, the risks you are willing to take, the values that are important to you, the people you associate with, the company you choose to work for, how you treat others—you own it!

And you give it everything you've got!

You don't let fear, worries or other people stop you or divert you from what you know in your Heart—and from what you really want deep down inside.

In business we have done a disservice to the Heart. We associate the Heart with emotions—and emotions equal weakness. We spend a lot of time trying to keep our Heart out of the workplace. Well that is the biggest mistake we can make!

Our mind is where we manufacture our fears, the nattering we experience—the "what ifs" for the future. We let our minds get in the way of our Heart, causing us to *react* to situations and detour us from what we know is true. We make concessions and accept mediocre behavior, lackluster results or even change our own aspirations, because we allow our own minds to convince us that the Heart is wrong.

Imagine for a minute if we did the opposite. We let our Heart guide where go. And instead, we use our minds to figure out how to get there! Isn't that what the great inventors, entrepreneurs and business leaders have done? Didn't they all listen to their Hearts and used their minds to make the impossible—possible?

That is being **All Heart!**

I am a dog person. For the last 8 years we had a special girl named Lilo. She had major issues most of her life. She had terrible hips and was probably in pain more than we ever knew. But she never let anything stop her. She ran and swam and lived life 100%. And even in her final days, she would run in her own way to bark a morning greeting at the neighbor dogs. Often doing this, she would fall—and she would fall hard. But she would just push herself up, shake her head and off she would go— running to bark at the dogs.

She knew what she wanted and she went after it.

She didn't let her mind lead her.

She didn't hesitate out of fear that she might get hurt or fall.

She didn't think about "what if."

She went all in—and **All Heart** every single day.

We can learn a lot from our dogs.

I choose to **Be All Heart** ...

8.6.15

# There's No Such Thing as Work Life Balance

The very term implies that there are two forces, battling each other out to see who wins our time, our focus—even our heart.

As professionals, we read many articles, books and blogs about finding a career that is our passion. Doing something we truly love. We need this!

And as human beings, we have family, friends, loved ones, and activities that we love—people and events that inspire and fulfill us. We need this too!

I am both a daughter and a wife.

I am a professional and a woman.

I am a dog lover and a friend.

I am a reader and a traveler.

I am not ONLY a daughter when I am with my parents. And I am not ONLY a wife when I am with my husband. I am all of these things at the same time.

There is no choice.

And there is no such thing as "Work/Life Balance."

There is only Balance.

There is only Efficiency.

There is just … Being!

There is a truth—we all only have 7 days a week and 24 hours each day. And everyday we have a choice how we spend that time.

At home or at work, crappy things happen. The car breaks down, an employee quits, the dog gets sick, you forward the wrong email. How we respond, how we react—all starts with Balance.

When the car breaks down, I can choose to rant, yell at my husband on the phone as I wait for the tow truck, and continue in the same defensive mood all day at the office. Funny how that ends up being a really bad day at the office!

When an employee quits unexpectedly, I can let it be the theme of every meeting and conference call that day, the subject of the dinner conversation with my spouse, and even continue in emails that night. Funny, that also ends up being a pretty sour night at home too!

But in either scenario, does this seem like an efficient use of my time? I had 24 hours that day—is a broken down car or an employee with a change of heart worth that much of my time?

What other things suffered that day because I CHOSE to not focus on them?

What did I miss in those other meetings or conference calls?

Do I even remember what I ate during that dinner last night? How would things have been different if I was "in the moment" instead of focused on things that had already happened?

Balance means we choose to focus on what is the most beneficial to ourselves and to others at the moment. Balance is about being ALL In and ALL Heart in whatever we are doing.

Efficiency is the amount of time, those precious hours in the day that we all have—how much time and energy we put into that focus.

The idea of work/life balance has become about "proving." We have to "prove" we are an ideal professional, parent, spouse etc. But in all this "proving," we lose sight of something important. We forget to BE. When do we focus on ourselves? To learn, to grow, to think, and to listen to our heart—that doesn't happen by scheduling 10 extra minutes in the day.

There is no magic formula for how to spend the hours of the day. But what I do know, is that the elements of my life that make me who I am are not separate little compartments, but are to be lived together.

What's important is to find balance as a person. To measure your own actions and responses. To know when you are being "inefficient" with your time at the expense of yourself and of others. To recognize if the time you are spending is either draining or inspiring. And to always seek Balance—to be fully present wherever you are focused.

As leaders, we cannot mandate a schedule that results in balance for others. Balance is a very personal thing. What we can do is demand, expect, and exude Efficiency. If you work well at night— make sure your team knows you don't expect the same from them. If an employee needs 10 extra minutes in the morning for his child's new school bus schedule—figure it out. Find the best way that is the most efficient for you and your team—and that leads to personal balance.

I haven't always been efficient. Like many of you, I have worked long hours when I probably didn't need to. One night this summer, I saw beautiful lightning bugs outside at our home. The woods seemed illuminated—it was beautiful. I commented to my husband this was the first year the lightning bugs were here. He looked at me funny—he said they are here every summer.

I guess I never saw them before.

I'm glad I see them now.

8.11.15

# Focus is Everything

A few months ago, I started walking. For years I made excuses that my schedule was too busy to find the time to exercise. But that was just an excuse—we can do anything if we really want to.

And one day, I just really wanted to walk.

I've become a bit obsessed with it. I'm fortunate to live near a beautiful park with trails and a lake. The scenery is breathtaking. I have been walking everyday for several months now. And in that time, I've learned a few things.

Each day I see a Blue Heron. They really are majestic creatures—rather prehistoric looking. They are a unique bird—equally comfortable on land, on water, and in the air. But when they are hungry, they fish.

I have watched this Heron stand ever so still—he slowly takes a step and pauses. He lifts one leg and slowly places it back down, gaining his balance. Then suddenly, he dives his head under water and brings up his catch.

He knew what he wanted—food—and he knew he needed to

strike at the exact moment to catch his dinner. He exerted just the right amount energy, no more, no less, to be successful. He was completely and utterly focused on his goal and on each literal step he needed to take in order to achieve it.

As human beings we all have goals. There are professional goals, performance goals, even goals of personal improvement. And sometimes, achieving the goal just seems overwhelming. It's easier to handle the "work" that needs to get done and just hope. We believe we are working hard; therefore, we are working towards the goal. We've convinced ourselves we're "fishing for dinner," like the Heron. Only for us—we're not catching any fish!

Imagine for a moment a world in which you are laser focused on your goal twice a day. Each day—once in the morning and once at night—you do nothing more than reflect on this goal and on the next step you need to take; not the entire process, but literally just the specific next step needed to achieve that goal.

**And then take that step.**

**No distractions.**

**No unneeded energy or movements.**

**Precision.**

**Focus.**

**Success.**

8.14.15

# Change—An Evolution

We think change is sudden. One day you have an employee, the next day he quits. One month we break sales records, the next month we don't. One day it's summer, the next it's fall. It's as if we believe change happens TO us—it's something we react and respond to.

But that's not really true. All change actually begins to unfold slowly overtime—we just don't see it. Did you know the leaves start to turn in August? I saw them on my walk today. Did you know that mallard ducks get darker this time of year? I saw them too. Why does this matter? Well, in the big picture it doesn't really. But weeks from now in mid-September, in the past—I would have said "Wow, it's fall already? When did this happen?" Meanwhile, the change had been happening for weeks ... slowly.

Employees don't just quit, business doesn't just suddenly fall off. All of these things happen but if we look closely, there were signals along the way slowly unfolding over time.

As leaders, it's up to us to watch for those signals.

To **anticipate** them.

To **prepare** for them.

And to **relish** in the anticipation of change.

With change comes **opportunity**.

And with it, we have two choices.

**React to it or Seize it.**

There is no in-between ...

8.25.15

# Lead Like an 8 Year Old

**Transparency. Authenticity. Innovation.** Are these just today's business buzzwords? Or do they represent something more powerful ...

When I was 8 years old—life was pretty simple. I played outside until the street lights came on and never spent a summer day indoors. And even in this young and simplistic life—there were a few things that were <u>REALLY</u> important to me.

**#1 The Real Scoop:** If I asked my mother why she said no to one of my requests—I really wanted an answer. "Because I said so" just didn't cut it anymore. I needed more. I wanted to know the real reason—and most of all, I needed to understand. *The desire to understand* actually became even more important to me than the fact that Mom had told me no.

**#2 Trust:** I'm sure we all remember that kid in school, we'll call her "Sally," who acted sweet to a classmate's face, but said mean things behind his or her back. We saw many different sides of "Sally"—nice to the teachers, mean to certain classmates, angelic with her parents. Sally had so many different "faces," we were never sure what was real and what was show. We learned early to stay clear of Sally and more importantly—to never trust her. We learned to *trust those who were consistent* no matter whom the audience.

**#3 Building on the old and creating the new:** As a kid, I was a pretty picky eater. Like most kids, I LOVED peanut butter (I still do). One day, not sure why, I put peanut butter on my waffles. I took two seemingly different things, put them together and created—Heaven! My mom was thrilled. Eating protein is pretty important for growing kids (and adults too). I had actually created a solution for a problem I didn't realize existed—getting me to eat more protein. Trying new things can lead to awesome solutions.

As adults, we are still like that 8 year old child. We have a need to understand. A desire to trust the people we work with and feel comfortable that we truly know who they are. And although change can be scary—deep down—we are motivated by the prospect of improving something and even get pretty excited about creating something brand new.

**Transparency, Authenticity and Innovation.** These are not new concepts. They are not buzzwords. Sure the words are longer, and sound a bit more intellectual. But we actually learned these important lessons many years ago.

*Tell the truth. Be honest. Be yourself. Work to improve. And never be afraid to try something new.*

9.7.15

# Be the Butterfly

I walk a few miles everyday in a park that is filled with butterflies.

Imagine starting life out as a caterpillar—a slow moving, slug-like insect. And through a metamorphosis—you are a beautiful winged creature, with the ability to fly and cover thousands of miles at great speeds! These two creatures could not be more different from one another and yet—they are one and the same.

This is the ultimate example of *Adaptability*.

I wonder, did the caterpillar worry about what life will be like as a butterfly? Did the butterfly wish he could go back to his life as a caterpillar?

Of course not!

Both remain focused on survival in the present—searching for safety, nourishment and an environment where they will thrive.

Are we really any different than the butterfly?

We all go through periods of metamorphosis in our lives—from babies to children; adolescence to adulthood; from young professionals to senior executives. And with each stage—<u>we evolve</u>.

Business goes through similar metamorphosis: horse-drawn carriages to autonomous vehicles; typewriters to computers; party-line telephones to smart phones.

Each day, we have a choice. We can choose to worry about things beyond our control; to live by the rules of the past—fighting to maintain the status quo.

Or choose to ... Be the Butterfly.

Embrace the Metamorphosis. Choose to Adapt. Focus on the Present and Prepare for the Future. Seek out ways to Nourish our bodies <u>and</u> our minds. Choose environments where we are not just safe—but where we grow and thrive.

I recently read a book called *"The Butterfly Effect."* The premise— when a butterfly flaps its wings on one end of the world, moving molecules of air—weeks later a hurricane occurs on the other side of the world. The idea is that all events are connected by seemingly unrelated events.

Each decision.

Each action.

Every word we speak—is like the butterfly flapping its wings.

The impact of our actions travels very far.

Be willing to Evolve.

Be Mindful everyday.

**Be the Butterfly!**

9.16.15

# Knowledge or Wisdom—Which do You have?

This morning I read a quote: "…knowledge is the facts and information you accumulate to inform you about a particular subject. Wisdom is what you do with it."—*Derek Lin*

There is one fundamental difference between these two— <u>ACTION.</u>

We spend the first 30% of our life in school—acquiring formal knowledge. And we believe this will take us somewhere.

Some of us even go on to pursue further knowledge—either in a formal academic setting, or on our own by continuing to read, study, and following specific trends. And we should—acquiring knowledge is very important and beneficial.

But then what?

Are we suddenly more capable?

Do we magically reach the pinnacle of success?

Knowledge is merely one tool in our toolbox. A hammer by itself can't build a house—it takes other tools, a plan, know-how, and people working together to build a solid structure.

Knowledge alone is not enough to take you … well anywhere!

What you do with that knowledge—the ACTIONS you take—that is the key.

The company where you choose to work, the people you surround yourself with, the career you create for yourself … these are all important decisions.

Problem solving … Hiring … Vision and direction … Culture … Strategy for growth … Exceeding client expectations … Involving the Board … Value for Shareholders …

All of these are the products of decisions you make, utilizing the many tools that you have—knowledge, experience, and instinct. But in the end, it's how you use your tools—it's the ACTIONS you take that actually build a business.

Knowing how to do something is important.

Actually DOING it—that's Wisdom!

9.23.15

# The Why Behind the How

Did you ever stop to think about WHY you do something? Why you act, or rather, REACT in the way that you do?

There are many things we do that are automatic. I bet when you brushed your teeth this morning—you didn't think about it at all. I know I certainly didn't. It's something I do each morning and evening and never really give it a thought. I decided (or more likely my mother decided for me) many years ago, that this was a good thing to do each day and I've been doing it ever since without a thought about it at all.

But what about in business? How often do we merely just *REACT* instead of *RESPOND*?

Is there a difference?

I think the difference is understanding the "WHY" behind our actions.

There are times we say something in haste, we send off a fiery email, or we just say "No" because it's the first thing that comes out of our mouths. There are practices and activities we continue because quite frankly, it's how we've always done them—and we don't even think about them anymore.

But when we RESPOND—we've taken time to consider. *We are mindful and deliberate in our actions and our communication.* It's not about the speed—it's about intent. Response can happen quickly—if you already know who you are, what's important to you, and are in tune with your personal values.

Quick decisions, articulate communication, diplomatic negotiations—are all required of leaders. The very idea of a leader is someone who paves the way, sets the tone, the direction and vision for the organization.

Being a leader is a lot about the HOW.

But before we can help others see the HOW, we must first be able to articulate the WHY to others—and more importantly—to ourselves.

Take a moment each day and look at the decisions you make, the words you use and ask yourself—what is my "WHY?" Spending time focused internally allows us to understand the "Why behind the How."

10.5.15

# Own The Understanding

We've all heard the expression "Communication is a two-way street." Meaning two individuals both participate and are equally responsible for the outcome.

I think this is wrong.

Communication is absolutely an exchange between people—sometimes two, sometimes many. But the responsibility is not shared. It is a sole responsibility. Whether with employees, coworkers or even your spouse—it is my responsibility to ensure the message I intend to convey is the message that is understood.

So often we say something, or more accurately—we THINK we said something—and yet what is understood is not at all what we were trying to say.

And what ends up happening? We blame the other person for failing to understand. When in reality, it was our own failure to clearly communicate our intended message.

This is particularly important when leading globally dispersed teams. As human beings, we use a lot of information to understand one another. We watch body language, facial expressions and connect to the tone of voice. But when dealing with teams across the country, or around the globe, often we only hear a voice on a phone or read from an email. Several of the cues we were taught to use are eliminated.

Since we were raised to use the whole picture to understand the meaning of communication—people tend to fill in the gaps for themselves. In the absence of some of these cues, they over analyze the words, read into the tone and interpret the silences as much as the words.

Those we are communicating with truly want to understand what we have to say. So why make it so hard? Why leave anything to chance or to question?

It is our responsibility, and ours alone, to ensure our intended message is understood. No assuming. No blaming.

As leaders, one of the most important things we can do is to take responsibility for the understanding of our own communication. Being a leader doesn't automatically mean you speak and others understand. If the other person does not react or perform how you intended—say to yourself "maybe I wasn't clear." If the other person doesn't "get it," change the specific language or the approach. Ask for input, ask for feedback and confirm everyone is on the same page.

Communication is a two-way street and leaders are the GPS on that journey. It's up to us to create understanding—and to find the right road so everyone is heading in the right direction.

10.11.15

# Is There Happiness at Work?

I had a boss many years ago that told me: "Your job should be fun, truly FUN, 80% of the time. The other 20% is the stuff you don't enjoy, could be things like—reports, hiring, firing etc.— whatever it is you identify as the junky part of the job. But 80%— should bring you pure joy, and yes—Happiness!"

We often hear the words "fulfillment, inspiration, growth, knowledge, challenge"—as things we seek from our jobs. And yet, it is rare that we associate the word "Happiness" with our work. That word tends to be reserved for times with our families, friends, community—basically the parts of our lives we spend OUTSIDE of work.

But why?

We spend more hours at work than we do in all of the other segments of our lives. Why should only portions of our lives bring us true happiness? Who would honestly only choose to be happy half of the time and merely tolerate, or worse yet—be unhappy the other half?

I think the word "Happiness" has fallen out of the workplace because we *feel* happy. It is one of the ultimate emotions. Being fulfilled, inspired, challenged—all imply something more intellectual and disconnected from emotions. But I believe it's when all of those other conditions exist, that we actually feel something.

A star football player is at his "Happiest" when he plays <u>the best he can</u> at the game he loves the most. If that same football player was on a basketball court—a game that may still challenge him but where he doesn't have the same natural talent or passion—he doesn't feel the same degree of happiness. In fact the opposite will probably happen. And no matter how hard the basketball coach may try, he can't make that football player happy on the basketball court. It's up to the football player to figure out he's playing the wrong game.

I have been very fortunate in my career to have periods of great happiness and joy in all aspects of my life—especially work. Sure there were "20% days," but there were many, many "80%" ones too. And when I found the scales tipping in the wrong direction— well that was generally time for me to make a change.

I believe happiness is something WE bring to our lives—all aspects of our lives. It's not something we feel part time or that happens TO us.

It starts with knowing who you are. What you are good at. What inspires and motivates you. It's knowing what your "80%" is—and the 20% too.

It's up to <u>you</u> to create an environment that produces the 80%.

Happiness is a choice. And we make that choice for ourselves.

There is "Happiness" at work.

We just have to feel it!

11.6.15

# Leadership is ...

I find business fascinating. Let's assume we have two companies that each produces a very similar product. The product itself is a quality product and let's also assume there is solid demand in the market for that product.

And yet one of our two hypothetical companies has stellar financial performance while the other is struggling. Why?

They both do the same thing, in the same market, with the same opportunities for success. So what makes one company perform better than the other?

Well, the first response is generally "management." But what does that mean? Does one company have "Superstar Management," while the other is managed by incompetent buffoons? Probably not. We have to assume both have highly competent managers at the helm. So then what is the real difference?

It's not about management ... it's about Leadership! Leadership isn't about the nuts and bolts of the company—that's management.

Leadership is about decisions, actions and inspiration. It's about creating a vision and bringing it to life for the people of the organization.

It's about instilling a belief in each and every employee of the company that we can and will do this together.

It's about listening to customers and planning for the future based on their needs—not your own.

It's about creating a culture that embraces the past while looking and acting for the future.

And it's having the courage to make decisions that deliver value for all—Shareholders, Customers and Employees, for today and tomorrow.

People define leadership in lots of ways. It's not easy to have one, nice compact definition.

But there is a truth …

Leadership is Impact.

Leadership is Legacy.

Leadership is about People!

11.12.15

# Hope is Not a Strategy and Worry is Not Execution

The other night my husband and I saw the movie "Bridge of Spies." In this movie, Tom Hanks plays James Donovan and Mark Rylance plays the Russian spy, Rudolph Able. It's based on a true story and chronicles the transfer of prisoners between the US and the USSR in the late fifties. Awesome movie—but this post isn't about the movie.

I keep replaying a line over and over in my head. Throughout the movie, as the case against Rudolph Able seems insurmountable, James Donovan repeatedly asks Able if he is worried. To which Able consistently replies, "Would it help?"

There are many events in life that cause us to pause. And in that moment—we have a choice. Often we imagine the worst and allow these scenarios to take root. We begin to worry, to doubt and to fear. Instead of envisioning the "possible" we allow our minds to only map out the *impossible*—and we then follow this course.

But what if in these moments we choose a different path? We imagine all possible scenarios and instead of worrying about what we cannot control, we think about what we will DO.

Visualize our actions.

Formulate a reasonable plan.

And then STOP.

Move on.

Bring our focus back to the present.

A football team prepares for a game by anticipating what their opponents will do on the field. They outline plays for a variety of scenarios. And then they stop. They don't worry. They don't fear. They are confident in their abilities. And they play the game …

Just as "Hope is not a Strategy," Worry is not Execution.

Science tells us we were not born with worry, doubt and fear.

We learned them.

We must ask ourselves—Does it Help?

11.30.15

# Do You have a Leadership Attitude?

There is a lot written about "PMA," Positive Mental Attitude. And it's true, even when you don't feel happy, if you force yourself to smile, pretty soon that smile becomes automatic and you just feel—happier!

I'm not sure organizations are much different. Let's face it, as leaders problems hit our desks everyday. And we make decisions to solve those problems; decisions that are necessary, important, and with far-reaching consequences. But focusing <u>only</u> on the problems and issues takes its toll. Suddenly, we assume <u>every</u> situation is fraught with challenges and we find ourselves focusing on what to fix—instead of on what to build!

Think of the great business leaders—they have some things in common:

They focused on possibility ... not impossibility.

They focused on decades ... not days.

They focused on others ... not themselves.

They Focused!

A Leadership Attitude is about Focus. I once heard Jack Welch say being a leader is like possessing a great light—and you decide where to shine it. That light is what will get all of the attention in the organization.

Focus the light on problems—everyone sees an organization filled with *Problems*.

Focus the light on solutions—everyone sees an organization filled with *Capability*.

Focus the light on the mission statement—everyone sees *Words*.

Focus the light on action—everyone sees *Results*.

Focus the light on people—everyone sees the *Heart* of the business.

Having a Leadership Attitude is understanding that your actions, your thoughts, even your very energy impacts everyone around you—family, coworkers, employees, customers, and shareholders.

Having a Leadership Attitude isn't really about you—it's about others. It's about shining your light, not for yourself, but to light the way for everyone around you.

Focus your light wisely. They are counting on you!

12.21.15

# Give the Best Gift—the Best You

The holidays are a time when many of us "recharge." People take time off to be with friends and family and step away from the usual pace of work. And this is important. A break in routine is always beneficial.

But these days I am noticing something different. My social media newsfeeds are filled with posts like: "I can breathe, I'm on vacation ..." or "Wow, freedom until the New Year..." or my personal favorite—"Away from the boss for two whole weeks ..."

These posts are not about spending time with family, holiday festivities or any of the others activities folks are looking forward to during the vacation time.

No, the tone is about escaping. It's negative. And it speaks of the underlying feeling at work—a lack of passion, inspiration, and fulfillment ...

We all love the idea of a vacation. But what is a vacation really? It's spending time with people we like, and doing things that make us feel fulfilled.

As leaders, we have to ask—what can we do to create that same spirit in the workplace? After all, we spend more time at work than we do at home. No, I'm not saying we need swimming pools and limbo games at the office. But can we create an environment that people don't need an escape from—but one in which our employees feel happy and fulfilled?

In the classic Christmas Carol, all Bob Cratchit really wanted was to feel valued—and maybe an extra piece of coal on the fire. Scrooge didn't need to do a lot <u>externally</u> to completely change Bob's world. It didn't cost money, or corporate resources. It was what he did <u>internally</u> that truly made the difference. It was a change in perspective and a realignment in priorities that allowed Ebenezer to become the person we all love at the end of the story.

During the holidays—while we are surrounded by friends and family, and reminded of what is truly important—let's keep our "work families" in mind too. Let's think about who we are, and <u>who we can be</u>, to make their lives, (and ours), more fulfilled.

Be a leader that people don't need to escape—but one they are honored to work with everyday!

The best gift you can give—is the Best of You!

1.1.16

# New Year's REVOLUTION!

Each year, many embark on New Year resolutions. These are generally things that we dislike, regret or are disappointed by and we "resolve" to change them.

How negative!

But a Revolution—well that's a whole different thing! When our forefathers planned the ultimate revolution, it wasn't out of regret or disappointment. They didn't decide to form our country because they were disappointed in their behavior the year before. Quite the opposite. They believed in themselves. They could see a better future. And they were determined to create that future for themselves and for those around them.

Isn't a personal New Year's REVOLUTION a much better way to start a New Year?

*Want to lose weight?* Don't just diet or join a gym. See yourself healthy and strong in the future and live each day contributing to that goal.

*Want to spend more time with your children?* See the fulfilling relationship you have with your kids and make the moments count everyday—from time in the car to time doing homework.

*Want a promotion or to grow in your career?* Don't wait for others to make you successful. Take control of your destiny and focus your actions everyday to impact others—and you'll blaze a trail of success for yourself.

A New Year isn't negative. It's not the time to focus on what you did wrong, what needs fixing, or the regrets of the past. A New Year is fresh, clean and new. It's like a puppy—all bright-eyed, curious about the world and completely fearless!

A New Year is a time of Opportunity.

A time of New Beginnings.

A time of Belief. Determination. And even Faith.

It's a time to remember <u>YOU</u> have the power to shape your future.

It's time for a REVOLUTION!

1.15.16

# Lead, Follow or Get Out of the Way!

I am a dog person. My husband and I were not blessed with "human children," instead we have "canine children!" And we don't just have any dogs—we have Newfoundlands. They are BIG, slobbery, hairy dogs with a lot of heart and *a lot of strength.*

Years ago when we got our first Newfoundland, we worked with a trainer. I knew if this dog was going to weigh more than I do and stand taller than me on two feet—well, I better be able to control this dog.

I will never forget one of the first things our trainer told us: "dogs will either lead or follow, they don't care which, but there is no in-between." He explained that in a pack, each dog has a role and at home you all form a pack. If a dog doesn't sense the presence of a leader, he will assert himself to lead, even if that isn't his most comfortable role. This is when you see dogs becoming destructive at home, chewing furniture, pottying in the house, aggressive towards others ... However, if the dog is comfortable with the leader, trusts the leader—he will happily follow him. This is a well-behaved and more importantly, a well-balanced dog.

I think the same can be true for humans. When we see unruly

children in a restaurant, is it really the kids' fault—or is it the parent's? And what about at work? Quite often, when we see "problem employees," instead of looking at the employee, we can look at the "leader," and see the real root of the problem.

Dogs can't read our minds or even sense tone very well. They tend to take everything at face value. We can't "test" them to understand us—we need to train them. One of the first things we did to teach our dog to come when we called, was to train on a 30-foot leash. He quickly learned he could explore the entire world around him—within 30-feet of us. He was able to challenge his mind, flex his senses, and yet he understood his boundaries too.

Sometimes I think we "test" our employees instead of "training" them. Are we waiting for them to reach our same conclusions? Do we use double-speak and hope for understanding? Do we assume? Are we clear in our meaning?

As leaders we must provide autonomy and the room to discover, to try new things and yes, to fail and to learn. But we also need to be transparent, honest, decisive, and clear about boundaries and our expectations.

As humans, we have a need to understand what is expected of us and a desire to follow others that are inspiring, challenging and confident. Not that different from our canine friends.

People will either Lead or Follow ... Which do you choose? It's up to you!

2.3.16

# Are You a "Quality" Leader?

I pride myself on being able to juggle a lot at once. A Lot. And never dropping a ball.

How many of us start our day with a list a mile long of things we need to accomplish and we just plow through that list, moving from one task to another as quickly as possible. Conference calls, emails, reports, errands, dinner, kids, more email ... We multi-task. Or as my husband refers to it: "Screwing up multiple things at once." (So what if most nights I burn the bread while cooking dinner)?

We move fast, and we work hard to get more and more crossed off that list. And at the end of the day, it feels good when we see lots of things fall off the list. We judge the day by the *"Quantity"* of our work.

Recently, I attended a meeting. This was one of those meetings with multiple departments and divisions; where each group presents an overview of their business. We've all been there. A lot of work goes into the preparation of each presentation.

This type of meeting has been happening for centuries. About 20 years ago, I attended a similar meeting, but with a few obvious differences. For starters, there was a lot of paper! Projected presentations hadn't been invented yet after all! There was bad coffee, and cookies on the break—and everyone was holding a copy of the report.

And they were present. They were asking questions. They were engaged. They were *In the Moment*!

Now fast-forward 20 years to that same meeting. There's a beautiful presentation with audio and animation projected on the wall. The same amount of pride and work went into the preparation of the report. But what do you see around the room? Yes the same bad coffee and cookies—but look at the people— what do you see?

Are they *present?* Are they *engaged?* Are they even making eye contact with the presenter?

No, most are looking at their phones or computers. Some are taking notes … And most are *"multi-tasking."*

When did "Quantity" become the mark of a leader? Think of the great leaders of our time. What do we remember about them? Do we think about the _number_ of letters Thomas Jefferson wrote—or the messages that were in them? Do we care _how many_ meetings Henry Ford attended—or do we care more that he enabled us to drive to work each day?

It's not the "Quantity" that made them great. It was the Impact they had on our lives that makes them memorable.

As leaders we have a lot of responsibilities. But our legacy will not be the "Quantity" of our work. It will be the "Quality." We won't be remembered for "multi-tasking." We will be remembered by the Impact we have on our organizations and more importantly— on others.

How do we create this Impact ?  Through interaction and introspection. By being present in meetings. By asking questions. By engaging with others. By Being in the Moment!

The other morning I was feeding my dog, Izzy. He's an old guy and has a medical condition that requires him to sit upright after he eats. I generally sit with him and pet him, but this particular morning, I was checking my email on my phone while he was sitting. He barked at me. Every time I touched my phone—he barked.

I put my phone down. He just quietly stared at me. And we sat there together. I was engaged. I was In the moment.

It's not "Quantity."

It's "Quality."

Thanks Izzy!!

Jennifer Hansen

# Chrysalis ...

Jennifer Hansen

2.10.16

# Season of Reflection

I was raised Catholic, and as a child Lent was a time of year to "give things up"—candy, fast food, soda ... But many years later, I don't think that was really the point.

In nature, many creatures take time to "pause." They hibernate, they rest, they migrate ... In the middle of winter, nature shifts its routine to build strength in preparation for Spring.

As leaders, it's important for us to also take time to "pause." We need to reflect—and to act; to build on our learning, and strengthen our character.

Instead of focusing on things to give up—wouldn't we all benefit by focusing on qualities or characteristics that make us better?

Whether Christian, Buddhist, Jewish or something else all together—we all benefit from taking time to reflect and renew ourselves. *Reflection is not about religion. Rather it is a necessity of leadership.*

*Author's note: The following passages were written daily during the season of Lent; as winter was trying to shift into spring. During my own "Season of Reflection."*

2.10.16

# Patience!

It's easy to be stuck in a routine and become frustrated when things don't move as we expect. Do you get frustrated when you are interrupted by a call? Do you find yourself sighing when a coworker comes into your office while you are working on a project?

I'm definitely a "List" person. I tend to follow a set routine—especially in the morning. This morning, before my coffee, I was outside with the dogs. It was cold and snowing and I wanted to come inside.

Suddenly two of my Newfoundland dogs, Izzy and Lani, were playing with each other. They were racing around chasing each other in the snow. To see the joy and happiness of these two senior-age dogs playing in the snow filled my heart. I would have missed this if I had rushed through my routine.

**Sometimes a little Patience brings us an unexpected gift!**

2.11.16

# Presence!

As leaders, as professionals, as parents, as friends, as human beings—it's important for each of us to "pause" and focus on the things that make us stronger, richer ... better.

I am a breakfast person. Some people like to skip it, but I need a bit of protein at the start of my day. In the morning, I juggle—a lot! I have 3 dogs to walk and feed, and walk again ... and again! I get myself ready for the day, catch up on the world's news, see what's happening in the stock market, check and respond to early morning email ... all before coffee. The list goes on.

One of my favorite morning meals are soft-boiled eggs. Making soft-boiled eggs is like a perfectly timed dance. The eggs must first be at room temperature. They must boil on a "soft-boil" for 5 minutes—no more, no less. And timing the toast and eggs to finish simultaneously—well that takes athletic prowess. I confess, some mornings I am not successful. While I attempt to cook my eggs, I read email, get dressed, go outside with a dog ... My presence is everywhere except with those eggs. And the result? The eggs are hard or undercooked all because of my lack of attention—my lack of presence.

Presence is having <u>both the mind and hand</u> operating in the exact same moment. It's having our focus on what we are doing right now—not on what's next or what happened in the past.

It's funny, the simple act of making eggs reminds me that being present, fully present, not only benefits others—but benefits me too.

My eggs were perfect this morning!

2.12.16

# Flexibility!

I start my day "ready for battle." I'm not an "ease into the day" kinda person. I have a "plan of attack" (a schedule) for the day. From professional meetings, to personal errands—there are things I plan, and generally accomplish everyday! It's amazing how successful one can feel by merely crossing things off of a list.

But then there are days when the whole agenda goes out the window. Something unexpected happens that demands your full attention. Yesterday was one of those days. We spent six hours in the emergency vet with one of our dogs. She is fine now—but it was a stressful (and scary) sort of day.

Someone often tells me (okay, that someone is my husband), "You are where you are supposed to be, doing what you are supposed to be doing." And you know what? He is right! Instead of being frustrated in traffic, at an airport, at work or even in a vet's office—being flexible opens you up to new experiences and new opportunities.

We met some very nice people at the emergency vet. They just wanted to chat as they waited anxiously for news on their pet. I'm glad we were there to talk with them. I hope we helped.

Be Flexible.

Sometimes something more important is waiting for you!

2.13.16

# Service!

I once heard an interview with Jack Welch, former Chairman of GE, where he described his job. He said he used his office, his title, the role he played at the company—not to focus on himself, but rather to call attention—to shine a light on others. And where he put his focus—others would naturally follow.

Not too long ago, I had to give an important presentation to about 300 people. I was preparing my speech and searching for the right words. A friend said to me: "Jennifer, don't tell them what <u>you want them to know</u> ... tell them what <u>they need to hear.</u>"

I can think of so many examples in my life, when I stopped worrying about what I wanted and focused on what someone else needed—and I ended up with more than I ever imagined. In serving others, I actually served myself!

Service gets a bad wrap. Some people think it means being weak or allowing ourselves to be taken for granted. That's not service.

*Service doesn't mean putting yourself second. It just means putting the other person first.* And you both win!

2.14.16

# Silence!

This morning, I walked outside with the dogs. It was completely silent. It was so silent that I noticed it! I looked out at the woods and the valley behind our home. Suddenly, it was like an image coming into focus. I saw the sun shining through the trees and the snow glistening like diamonds. And then the sounds began. I slowly heard all different kinds of birds chirping, the wind gently blowing. As I walked, my own footsteps were suddenly deafening.

In the silence, beautiful sounds and images gradually appeared.

We tend to think we need to have all of the answers— immediately. We need to be first to speak or to act. But if we just start talking, what else do we miss?

How do we find the right words or uncover new ideas?

By observing. By hearing. By feeling.

**Listen in the Silence. It's amazing what we hear!**

2.15.16

# Heart!

Heart. We saw a lot of hearts yesterday on Valentine's Day. Heart is a word and image associated with love, emotion, our pets, our kids, our families. All that is dear to us ... personally.

But when we look at our whole lives—the work we do, the businesses we are in, the transactions we conduct—somewhere along the way we've been told the heart is not welcome. "Leave your feelings at the door" is something we've all heard before. Heck, I've even said this!

But today, I have a different view of things. I don't think the problem is with the heart or our emotions. It's a question of balance. I have to balance what I am feeling with how to make it happen!

Think of some of the greatest leaders of our time—from Mother Theresa to Steve Jobs. They all first had a feeling. A spark coming from the heart. Did they extinguish it? Did they work hard to smolder that feeling? Absolutely not.

**They listened to their heart—and then used their mind to bring that dream to life.**

The Heart plays an important role in ALL aspects of our lives. Instead of ignoring it—let's invite it into the room.

It may have something important to say!

2.16.16

# Determination!

I like to win—who doesn't? Some might even say I'm pretty competitive (just ask my Fitbit Buddies)! But Determination is something different. We all have goals—professionally and personally. From landing a big account to losing 20 pounds—that is the "What." But Determination goes one step further—it's about the "Why." **And more importantly, it's all about YOU and no one else.**

You can't be determined for someone else. Determination is a very personal thing. I've had the pleasure to coach and train a lot of people. I've taught people how to negotiate, how to hire, how to grow revenue—even how to potty-train dogs ... the list goes on. I can teach the "How" of a lot of things. But I can't teach the "Why."

The "Why" is what is inside of <u>YOU</u>. It's what makes you <u>want</u> to do something. It's a fire in your belly. **And that fire is Determination.**

We sometimes rely on others for our determination. We look to our family, friends, even our spiritual community to provide us with our determination. Each is very important in our lives. And each gives us very important tools—but the tools are the "How" in getting to our goals.  Simply having a car filled with gas doesn't get you to your destination. It takes more than that.

It's up to you to find your "Why."

Stay Determined!

2.17.16

# Simplify!

More!

Less!

We associate success, happiness, fulfillment—with "MORE." More room in our homes, more clothes in our closets, more money in our bank accounts, more friends, more vacations, more jewels, more cars ... **"MORE" equals happiness.**

And we associate "LESS" with things that are sub-par, falling short, not meeting expectations, lacking, it's negative ... **"Less" equals want.**

But it's not the words—it's our understanding that is backwards. Let's flip these words around for a minute ...

Less on our schedules leaves MORE time for our family, friends and ourselves.

Less in our closets means MORE room to actually see the clothes we own.

Less "things" in our homes means MORE room to breathe and recharge.

Less food on our plates means MORE reasonable eating and healthy living.

Less time indoors means MORE time outdoors.

Less of quantity leaves room for MORE quality.

More is not better—Less is not worse. It's a matter of perspective.

About eight months ago, I started to "Simplify." I cleaned closets, started eating differently, spent time outdoors everyday; and I made an important discovery.

As I focused on "Less"—my life became filled with "More."

**Choose to Simplify.**

**You're not getting Less.**

**You're gaining More.**

2.18.16

# Confidence!

I read an article the other day that asked the question: "Do we *value people because of their past ... or because of their potential?"*

I think sometimes we let experience trump confidence.

When we think of our own capabilities—we look at our experience. We start with the things we have done well in the past and assume that defines our capabilities. But are we really being fair to ourselves? Is our potential completely defined by our past—or are we capable of doing more?

As human beings we are faced with the "known vs. the unknown." And naturally, we tend to gravitate towards what is known. We buy the same brand of peanut butter because we know we like it. We choose a fast food restaurant because we know what it will taste like. We choose the same brand of clothing because we know it fits well. And most of all, we challenge ourselves to the limits of what we have done before—instead of what we are capable of doing now!

None of us are the same person today that we were years ago.

Pick a point in time 10 years ago, even 2 years ago. Everyday since then, we have learned new things and acquired new skills. Why then do we limit ourselves to thinking we are only capable of performing and accomplishing to the level we did in the past?

Why? Because of fear. We don't want to fail, make a mistake, disappoint others ... or ourselves.

Confidence is believing, when faced with the "unknown," we can figure it out. And if things don't work out? Well, we continue to learn and acquire more skills—developing in new ways.

**Confidence may be born in experience.**

**But it is defined by potential.**

2.19.16

# Change!

I am a creature of habit. I generally sit in the same seat in any meeting, I typically order my favorite dish at my favorite restaurant, and I have the same basic routine each morning as I start my day. You could say—I follow a predictable path.

But every once in a while, it's important to change. I've been reading a bit about Feng Shui. Considered both an art and a science, Feng Shui has been studied for more than 3,000 years and connects nature, to our environment, to us. It focuses on energy and being aware that **nature is ALWAYS changing. And with it, we must change too.**

I think the lessons found in Feng Shui go much further than what color pillows should be on the couch, which direction the front door should face, or where to place a water fountain in the office.

I think the true message is that change is natural. The wind blows, the water flows, and nothing in nature stays completely the same forever. **Nature doesn't fight change—it adapts to it— and even embraces it!**

This morning I noticed a big pine tree at our home. It's very tall and has been here longer than I have been alive. The wind was blowing hard, and I watched the top of the tree bend and flex to the wind.  As I looked further down the trunk of the tree, it was stable and grounded in the earth. The tree has adapted over time. It takes advantage of the changing seasons and the changing environment to continue to grow and thrive.

Just imagine if that tree fought the change. If it didn't bend and flex with the wind, it would grow hard and brittle and eventually break and die.

We have a choice each day.

As the winds of change blow, we can fight it and break, or we can adapt and grow like the tree.

*I love trees!*

2.20.16

# Breathe!

It's Saturday. The sun is shining, the wind is blowing, and it feels like a perfect Spring Day. I have the windows open at our home letting the fresh air flow throughout the house. You can almost hear the house take a big sigh as the fresh air comes in and the stale air from the winter flows back outside.

Breathing is such an automatic response that we forget about it. But every once in a while, we appreciate this amazing sense—like when we smell cookies baking, the scent of new leather boots or even the fragrance our grandmother used to wear. Taking a breath causes us to pause—and to get lost in a particular moment.

We get caught up in our daily lives. From conference calls to car pools—it seems we are always moving at 100 mph. But when things are really busy, or a situation is tense, or the future feels uncertain—we have an amazing gift. All we need to do is breathe. Not just ordinary, breathing to exist, kind of breathing. **Close your eyes, and really BREATHE!**

Suddenly ... the world slows.

You feel grounded.

You feel balanced.

You feel in control.

Suddenly—the situation seems better.

And all you did ... was breathe!

If all that can happen with just one breath—imagine what else you are capable of doing!!!

2.21.16

# Experiment!

To me—experimenting is different than changing. To change is to make a decision. It's a conscious choice to do one thing or another. You eat chicken, or you switch to beef. You have blond hair or brunette. Change denotes an "either/or" situation.

But experimenting is something different. It's not about change—it's about an *experience*. It's putting yourself in a situation that you have never been in before—in order to then make a decision. And yes that decision may lead to change—or it may not. But you will never know unless you are willing to experiment.

We often associate "experimenting" with science or technology and people who make their living trying to create new solutions. And yet, it's important for all of us to experiment. Everyday we are faced with decisions in our personal lives and in our professional lives—from politics, to sports, to food, to how we raise our kids and how we train employees.

But instead of relying on others to tell us how we should act, feel or respond—we need to make our own decisions. It's important to experiment, try new things, have discussions with new people—and then make our choices.

We are each the inventors of our own life.

Don't be afraid to experiment.

You may just discover something amazing!

2.22.16

# Faith!

The older (and hopefully) wiser I am becoming—I know there is not really a difference between our professional and personal selves. Who we are inside, the best we are as individuals, that is the person we need to be at the office and at home. With the same beliefs, the same values—and yes even the same language.

Faith was not a word previously used in a business setting. Words like "faith and love ..." well those were "emotional" words and we were taught they didn't have any place in business. And since "faith" can have different meanings to different people—we shouldn't use it because it might offend someone.

I think that's wrong. Faith is a powerful word—and I think it belongs in every aspect of our lives.

Faith is not about religion.

It's not blind acceptance.

It's not an absence of accountability.

Faith is a belief that when we make a decision, the outcome will be exactly what was supposed to happen, even if different than what we expected.

Faith is an understanding that our words, actions, even energy, impact others beyond our own comprehension.

Faith is knowing events are happening in the world and in our lives, even when we can't see them.

And Faith is the knowledge that we can handle any situation that comes our way.

What is Faith?

**Faith is Strength.**

**Faith is Courage.**

**Faith is Being Fearless!**

2.23.16

# Open!

Being open can be a struggle for a driven individual. We have a goal in mind, we have the determination to reach that goal, and we lay out a plan to achieve it. And then we hit—GO! Nothing distracts us or stands in our way of achieving our goals!

And there's nothing wrong with that. In fact, following that strategy has worked for me over and over in my personal and professional life many times.

Being open doesn't mean we stop doing what makes us great. Being open adds a layer to this strategy.

Think about a window. It's primary purpose in a room is to let in light and provide a view to the outside world. Now—open the window. It still does everything it was designed to do—only now it is also letting in fresh air! Nothing has changed and yet the whole experience in that room has changed. It smells better, it feels fresh—the energy is different.

I think that is what being Open is like for us. We have goals and plans, and yet we need to let in fresh ideas and experiences. Sometimes it enhances our plans. Other times, it may cause us to change them all together. If we set our sights too closely on just one outcome or plan, we may miss something even greater along the way!

Be Driven.

Be Determined.

And remember to open the windows!!

2.24.16

# Fearless!

I am not a daredevil. I will probably never bungee-jump, I don't like roller coasters, and skydiving is definitely not in my future. But is that what being Fearless means?

I can think of some amazing people from history: Gandhi, Oskar Schindler, Mother Theresa ... I would say they were "Fearless."

Did they have superhuman strength? No.

Did they make mistakes? Probably.

Did they have doubt? I bet they did.

They were human ... and FEARLESS.

I think the emotion of fear is learned and not innate. In the wild animals don't exhibit fear—they feel threatened and respond. When a wolf is threatened—it may attack or it may run away, depending on the degree of the threat. There is no worry, no doubt—it is decisive action based on given circumstances. It makes a rationale decision to preserve its life—and to be what it was born to be—a wolf.

Think of a child afraid of the dark. The child may have heard that the Boogey Man lives in the dark. It's as if one day the child is not afraid, and suddenly, because of this new "knowledge," the child now believes the dark is something to fear.

When we feel fear in our lives, it's because we learned it along the way. Think of the things that you are most afraid of: public speaking, dealing with illness, making a mistake, losing your job … Why are we afraid of these things? Because somewhere, someone, told us it is in these moments that the Boogey Man lives.

Be Fearless. Just as at some point we all learned there is no Easter Bunny (sorry if I just burst that for some), we can also all learn that there is no Boogey Man. There wasn't in the dark, and there isn't now.

We make decisions throughout our lives. We react or we don't to circumstances as they come our way. But being Fearless means, no matter what, we make decisions that make us better, and that we stay true to ourselves and most of all—to who we were born to be.

Just like the wolf!

2.25.16

# Gut!

Are there things you just know? They come so naturally to you that you don't even need to think about them—it's automatic?

Some people refer to this as intuition, others call it a feeling or sixth sense, and some (like me)—just call it Gut!

In our personal and professional lives—we are faced with decisions everyday.  Some are minor, like what to wear in the morning or what to make for dinner tonight.  Others are more important—like how to answer a question during an interview or who to hire for a particular position.

Think of some of the greatest leaders of our time. What makes them great can largely be defined by the decisions they made throughout their careers. Decisions to do or not do something, to invent something new, to try a new strategy, to stop or to start—it all comes down to decisions.

How do we make decisions? Well, we call upon our experience. We look to our education and academia to inform us. And we rely on others as advisors, counselors and friends. But in the end, in a singular moment when we say: "Yes, this is what I believe"—

where does that come from? It comes from your Gut!

Have you gone back after you made a decision to review how it worked out? Think about the various times when you made a decision and things went well—what was your gut saying to you prior to making that decision? Now, how about the times that things didn't go as planned—what did your gut say to you prior to that decision?

Gut is not an accident. It is not luck. It's not magic.

Gut is not attached to a particular outcome.

Gut is strength.

Gut is intellect.

Gut is faith.

Gut is experience.

Gut is part of YOU.

You just have to listen!

2.26.15

# Compassion!

As human beings—we often need to share (what we perceive), as bad news. We need to tell someone they didn't get a job, are being fired or that they really messed up a big project.

We perceive delivering bad news as our "fault." We take on the responsibility for the other person's happiness and unhappiness. We assume that since our news is going to leave them feeling bad—we are somehow to blame. And maybe if we prolong telling them, avoid it completely, change it, soften it ... well then they won't feel as bad and in the end—we won't be at fault.

But is that really being compassionate? That sounds like an awful lot of ego to me. We put way too much emphasis on ourselves in these scenarios instead of the other person. Is being compassionate protecting ourselves from blame? Of course not.

Being compassionate isn't about feeling sorry for someone, or just being nice. Compassion is speaking and acting from our hearts—and doing <u>what is best</u> for others and for ourselves.

When we have to let an employee go—being nice or feeling sorry for him may lead you to let him coast. But being compassionate is helping him discover that he has amazing talents in other areas and there is something better out there for him.

Sharing with someone that she made a big mistake isn't about blame. So often we focus on HOW the mistake happened. Who cares? It happened. What is much more important is the WHY. Did the employee not understand? Did she lack confidence? Was she given bad direction? Being compassionate isn't about finding fault—it's about teaching, learning and finding solutions.

Being compassionate isn't being soft or weak.

Being compassionate is about strength ... and love.

Being compassionate is doing what is best for the other person.

*Which is always best for us too!*

2.27.16

# Today!

When I was five years old, I used to love watching Happy Days followed by Laverne and Shirley on Tuesday nights at 8pm. But when the shows were over, I had to go to bed. My mom told me "when you get older, you can stay up later." I couldn't wait for that to happen.

When I was in school, I looked forward to a lot of things. I couldn't wait to learn the next subject, drive a car, go to prom, be able to vote … There was always something I was waiting for, something not only to aspire to, but would ensure my place in society and with it—my happiness.

As adults we have experienced most of what we were waiting for as children and yet that feeling of anticipation still exists. Whether it's landing a big account, going on a big vacation, buying a particular car, living in a certain neighborhood—we pine for a specific outcome and timeline—and attach our happiness to it.

Several months ago, my husband and I were in Boston for my graduation from MIT. For two years, there were classes to balance with a job, assignments, tests, projects, travel, and then the graduation itself.

On this particular Sunday, the festivities were now over and there was nowhere we had to be. It was a beautiful day—blue skies, warm but not hot—the perfect day to just be.

We joined a friend of ours and his 4-year-old daughter. The four of us explored the city. We rode in a horse drawn carriage, took a spin on a carousel—even had ice cream at the wharf. And at one point during the day, trotting behind that horse, I looked at my husband and my dear friend and thought to myself—there is nowhere I would rather be—I am completely and utterly happy right in this very moment!

My husband and I will be moving for the next phase in my career. A new city, a new job, new friends … There will be a lot of exciting change this year. And when big change is brewing, it is easy to attach your happiness to the future.

But in the past year, I have learned that happiness is not a destination. It is something to see, taste and smell right this very moment.

**Happiness is Today!**

2.28.16

# Humility!

**Humility is born in confidence.** Think of the most humble people you know.  They are confident in their own abilities, speak factually about these abilities—and yet it never feels like they are boasting.

When you are confident—there's no need to boast. It's just something you know to be true about yourself. **Confidence stems from certainty.** Like you know if you have blue eyes, are good at math—or can lead a group of people.

But being cocky is different. **Cockiness comes from uncertainty.** We've all met people that are cocky—they are loud and feel a need to tell the world just how awesome they are! We see this in politics, in business, even in friends and family. My husband has an expression (taken from an old song): "It's not the whistle that makes the train go."

And that whistle is cockiness.

But cockiness is short-lived. The uncertainty creeps back in and has a way of reminding us what is truly important.

Yesterday, my husband and I went trap shooting. For those not familiar, this is when someone calls "Pull," a sporting clay flies in the air, and you break it with a shotgun.

My first couple rounds were awful. But then I took a third try. And suddenly, they started to break. First one, then the next ... This was fun! I started to move faster. I looked at my husband to make sure he was watching—certainly I was destined to be a trap shooting all-star! 7,8,9 in a row broke! Then it was time to switch to the next position. And the inevitable happened. I missed—first one, then the next and the next after that. My streak was over.

I had been feeling cocky—not confident—and there was certainly no humility in my actions. Did I know why I was hitting well? Not really—I was just caught up in my own "awesomeness!"

That little streak showed me I might have ability—but I lacked understanding. I started to really pay attention. With each of the next shots—I learned just as much (if not more), from the missed shots than the ones when I actually broke the target.

**Being humble is a quiet confidence in what you know— and more importantly—in what you don't!**

2.29.16

# Values!

We learn right from wrong as very young children. And we learn this by how others respond to our actions. When we threw a tantrum or told a fib, our parents scolded us. When we shared our toys with our cousins, we were praised for being kind children. **We learned early to shape our behavior and our words—based on how others reacted.**

At some point a few years later, the sense of right and wrong starts to shape our personal values. **And it becomes less about how others will react and more about what feels right inside.**

When I was about 12 years old, I was on a basketball team. Our team was playing the toughest team in the league. It was a close game and we were all playing our hearts out. A friend of mine was on the opposing team. She got the ball on a rebound and was heading for her team's basket. As she started to dribble towards their basket, she tripped and fell—hard. I suddenly had the ball in my hands. I was wide open all the way to the basket and this was our chance to score. When I looked back, I saw my friend on the ground—crying in pain. And in that second I knew what I wanted to do—I dropped the ball, ran back to my friend, and helped her up.

I don't remember if we won or lost that game that day. But I knew in that moment, taking care of my friend was more important than scoring while she was down (literally).

There are some that still behave like young children. They speak, act, and operate based solely on how others will respond and not on what they believe to be right. *They make decisions out of fear*—wanting to avoid anything negative and striving for constant praise. They aim to please everyone—and lose themselves in the process.

Values are personal. They have nothing to do with how others will react and everything to do with our own beliefs.

When we make decisions based on our values we do so, not because it is popular, **but because we know it is right.**

3.1.16

# Bravery!

Our youngest Newfoundland dog, Lani, is what you would call "bomb-proof." Nothing much rattles her or scares her. She faces the world with certainty and when she encounters something new, she pauses to process the situation and then moves forward with confidence.

This morning was something different. We have a balcony off of the sunroom at our home, where the dogs sometimes enjoy the fresh air. But today, Lani flatly refused to go out onto the balcony. She was visibly afraid and didn't want to even take a step onto the deck. I immediately wondered—what happened in the past that is making her afraid now?

But then I realized—it doesn't matter what happened previously. Whatever happened was in the past and those conditions don't exist today. All that matters is right now and getting her to move forward.

I think we are a lot like this. When we are unsure of ourselves, or uncomfortable in a situation, we let past experiences dictate how we feel—instead of just moving forward and experiencing something new, today, right now!

It didn't take us long to encourage her on the deck. And pretty soon, Lani was walking in and out of the doors on her own without any encouragement at all. She was the same, brave, confident girl we were used to seeing.

Bravery isn't a feeling—it's an action. It's recognizing that whatever we experienced in the past is just that—past.

And the only option we have ... is to move forward!

3.2.16

# Inspire!

**Inspire—it's a verb.** Not to be confused with the adjective "inspired." The adjective is about ourselves, but the verb—well that is something we do for others!

Do you ever stop to think how your daily activities inspire others? We are all busy and caught up in our own lives, but boy, when someone goes out of their way, even doing something simple—it really makes a difference.

Last night, my husband and I stopped to grab dinner at a local chain restaurant. This was not a "night out" kind of evening—it really was just food. We had just come from the vet clinic where one of our dogs is in the hospital. It was a stressful evening, we were both feeling pretty blue and neither of us felt like cooking.

The food was predictably good, but certainly not fine cuisine. What stood out to both of us was the service. Our server was friendly and attentive, but it was the manager that changed our evening. After the meal, the manager came over to ensure we had a good evening—but he didn't just give us a canned speech like we all have experienced in the past. No, this gentleman thanked us sincerely for coming in to the restaurant and said how glad they were that we chose that restaurant last night. But it wasn't his words—it was his energy. He had a smile that came from his eyes and filled his entire face. When he spoke, he was truly interested in us—he even put his hand on his chest in a humble gesture. It was as if he was personally thanking us for coming to his home.

The smile, that energy, made a real difference. Suddenly, I was smiling back. That manager had no way of knowing what kind of day we had—but being so warm, sincere and genuine—well, we both walked out of that restaurant feeling a lot better than when we had walked into it.

Being an inspiration to others doesn't mean you are saving lives, inventing things, or giving sage advice. Sometimes a smile filled with compassion is inspiration enough.

**Choose to inspire today!**

3.3.16

# Empty!

What does it mean to be empty? For the longest time, this word felt negative to me. It conjured up the idea of being devoid of emotion, lacking interest or energy. Being empty was the same as feeling spent ...

The opposite of empty is full. Let's say you feel like a glass of milk. You reach for a glass, but it's already filled with orange juice. Clearly you can't use that glass—it's not empty. And that glass of orange juice remains full until you drink it, or spill it—but either way, it's full and not of any use to you right now. If you really want milk, you need an empty glass to enjoy your beverage.

I think we spend a lot of time being "full." We become attached to a particular outcome or the way we think things are supposed to be. We become so focused on the end result that we lose sight of what is really important.

In my beverage scenario—what is really the most important thing? Some would say the milk. Others may even say the orange juice. But the most important thing is the empty glass—you can't enjoy the milk or the juice, without first starting with an empty glass.

Being empty is not negative at all. It has nothing to do with a lack of emotion or energy.

Being empty is a confidence in who you are. Just like that glass—sometimes you hold juice, other times milk—but it's in being empty that you provide the greatest service.

3.4.16

# Learn!

They say, "An old dog can't learn new tricks." Well as a dog person—I know this is not true. And it certainly isn't true with people either.

Several years ago, we had a mutt named Montgomery. He came from the pound and was an amazing dog. He was obedient, loving … really the best dog. Except for one thing—he didn't like other dogs. At the time, neither my husband nor I knew anything about dog training or dog behavior. We just modified everything around him—we made sure Montgomery was never with other dogs and we didn't take him anywhere. We thought, "This is just the way Montgomery is …" and believed he could never be different—and he could never learn.

I think we do this in our lives too. We accept the things we are not good at, or things about ourselves we wish were different, as "*This is just the way I am.*" We've convinced ourselves we are beyond changing … and beyond learning.

But that is just an excuse. We learn new things all of the time. From technology to nutrition, we've gained a lot of new knowledge over the years. Think back to when you graduated school. You've learned a lot since then about business, about life … about yourself. *"Learn something new everyday"* is not just an expression—it's fact.

Then why do we just accept some things as *"This is just the way I am"* and believe we can't learn to be different?

I think it's because we're afraid. The things we accept about ourselves are really the things that bother us the most. We wish we could change—but we are afraid we will fail trying.

Whether you want to lose weight, learn to cook, be a better public speaker or even be more confident—there is ALWAYS something to learn and always a way to improve. And if you fail? Who cares! Transformations are never immediate!

Learning doesn't start and end in a classroom or in a book.

Learning is about desire.

A desire to change.

A desire to understand.

A desire to be better.

And we are never too old to be better!

3.5.16

# Calm!

This morning the family of deer that live on our property came for a visit. They are so graceful. As I watch them walk quietly and precisely through the woods—I always feel a sense of calm. Their natural quiet, yet deliberate energy, is infectious.

When something confronts a deer that she doesn't like—she calmly lets us know. She stands assertively, stares intently at us, and slowly stamps a front foot. It's the same calm energy—just channeled in a very specific direction. And if the deer senses danger—she uses that same calm energy to get away.

The deer doesn't chatter to the other deer when things don't go as planned. She doesn't run around in circles screaming or ranting and getting all of the other deer excited or upset. No, she remains calm—and focuses her energy in a way that serves her best.

We can learn a lot from nature. Does it help when we get upset? When an account is lost, the dinner is burned, a mistake is made—how do we react? Rant and rave, maybe even yell and scream, or vent to whomever will listen? What good does that do?

Not only do we get upset, but so does everyone around us. And pretty soon, our own energy has created an environment of fear, distrust, and anxiety in everyone else. That doesn't sound like energy well spent for ourselves—or for those around us.

Every day we have a choice.

We don't *have a bad day*—we *choose to see and react to the day badly* and waste our energy on things that don't serve us well.

We don't *have a good day*—*we choose to see and react to the day in a positive way* and focus our energy on things that are beneficial.

It all starts with a choice.

Being calm is a choice.

Make your choice!

3.6.16

# Relax!

How do you relax? Some people relax by taking a vacation, playing a round of golf, or boating. To relax is to escape.

For most people, relaxation happens during "down time," while they are not working. Relaxing is something we plan to do in the future, and it's scheduled like any other obligation, for a specific time or location. Only, when that future moment arrives, we never find the relaxation we were seeking—instead we are just as stressed as in everyday life. I bet if we visited a golf course, we would find people playing that are anxious, frustrated—even upset. And I thought this was supposed to be a time to relax?

Yesterday, my husband and I went to a Sporting Clays Tournament. We are new to the sport so we were just watching and learning. We noticed one of the shooters. He was pacing, waiting for his turn. He muttered to himself: "my nerves are getting to me." He was clearly not relaxed, he was anxious, worried, and tense—and he was not enjoying himself. After he shot, he said to us that he had only been shooting for seven months. He said it used to be fun—now it just feels like work.

I bet he started the sport as an escape. A way to get away and

154

"relax." Only he forgot something really important—to relax! He was repeating the same pattern from his everyday life. He was trading one situation for another—the environment may be different but his stress level was not.

Relaxation cannot be scheduled. It's not about a time or a place—**it's a state of being.** It's sort of like happiness. If I said I was going to *schedule* a time to be happy this Saturday—well that sounds ridiculous! You would ask—why wait until then? Be happy right now!

Relaxing is the same thing. It's a choice we make everyday. We can choose to approach each moment anxious and tense or we can be at peace no matter what we are doing.

Maybe if we spent more time finding a way to BE relaxed we wouldn't need to escape from life—we would actually live life!

3.7.16

# Results!

Many of us are very results-oriented. And that's a good thing. It means we are driven to deliver a certain outcome. At work—it may be the volume we produce or the revenue that is delivered. At home—it could be the quality of the dinner or the number of chores we get done in a weekend. We place the value on the actual result.

It's always about the finish line.

But what about the actual race? HOW are we achieving these results? Do we ever stop to think about the <u>process</u> instead of just the outcome?

Everything we do, from brushing our teeth to running a business, has a process. Understanding the steps in that process, those that work for us and those that need to change—that is where the results are born.

My great grandmother was an amazing cook. She was Slovak and made many traditional dishes "from the old country." One of her specialties was a pastry we called Nut Roll. It was a rolled yeast dough with a sweet nut mixture swirled throughout.

I've had lots of other nut roll in my life. I can even buy it at the grocery store. But it's never the same. Sure they are all considered nut roll, but the results are different.

There was something in my grandmother's technique that made her nut roll just a little bit sweeter, a little more flavorful. Her result was better. Unfortunately, we don't know what she did that made her nut roll so good. *We put all of the value on the result and never paid attention to her process.* And now—no one can repeat it.

When results are positive, we often don't pay attention to how we got there, we just enjoy the victory. We focus on the final score of the game instead of how the game was played. But then how do we repeat the win in the next game?

And when things don't go as expected—we often go to the opposite extreme and assume everything is broken and try to change too much at once. And when the results are still poor—we're even more confused.

Focus on the process—why it works, why it doesn't. Fix the things that need fixing and repeat what is working. When the process is right—the results will follow.

**Results are not the end of the game—they are a by-product of the game.**

3.8.16

# New!

When we are kids—so much around us is new. We begin playing a musical instrument, we take up a new sport, learn a new subject in school. It's as if every year—we discover something new.

And then we enter adulthood. We buy a home for the first time, we start a new career, we get married, have the first child ... There is a whole different set of "new" in this stage of our lives.

And then it feels like life settles down. Instead of figuring out how to do something for the first time—we start to feel comfortable and experienced. Life becomes more routine and predictable. And there is a comfort in this predictability.

But there is also a danger.

All those years ago, when we were tackling new things, we were learning and challenging ourselves. We were routinely out of our comfort zone—whether we liked it or not—and it was in those times that we grew.

- When we failed at the new sport we were playing, we learned focus and to block out anything that distracted us.

- When we blundered a new musical piece on our instrument, we learned to slow down during practice—timing is everything.
- When we were disappointed in losing the negotiation on our first house—we learned that everything happens for a reason—better things are generally around the corner.

Living a predictable life may feel comfortable but it's stagnant. And just like in nature—nothing thrives in stagnant water.

New ... challenges us.

New ... teaches us.

New ... develops us.

There is never a time in our lives when we "know it all." There is always something to learn or discover.

**Each day find the New.**

**Each day Strive to Thrive!**

3.9.16

# Evolve!

Oh. My. Goodness! It feels like spring today! The sun is shining, the breeze is blowing! As I walked one of my dogs this morning, I could hear the orchestra of birds singing all around me. It was as if they too were celebrating the arrival of spring.

I am often inspired, encouraged and taught by the things I see in nature. Today is no exception.

Many of the flowers at our home are starting to poke through the earth. They aren't new; they have been there all winter hidden under the ground. Building, restoring, growing—just waiting for the perfect moment to pop through the dirt. They will continue to grow and fortify until it's time for them to flower. But each day—they continue to evolve—and transform into something different.

As people—change is difficult. Some resist it, others avoid it, some deny it—and still others fear it. Even people who say, "I love change," don't love it all of the time. In many ways we do everything we can to keep things just as they are instead of embracing the seasons of change.

Nature is a great teacher. The flowers don't resist change—they flourish with it. They don't fight to stay in the ground—they fight to evolve!

Go outside and enjoy the beautiful day—even for a moment.

Take a deep breath.

Listen to the breeze.

And recognize—it's your time to bloom!

3.10.16

# Refresh!

Think about the last time you waited for a page to load while on the computer. For some reason, the page was stuck, the pictures weren't downloading, and you had the endless "hourglass" circling on your screen. At first you were annoyed. And then, what did you do? You hit the refresh button. The computer went back a step or two, it moved in a different direction, and when it came back to the page, everything worked just fine.

Albert Einstein once said *"doing the same thing over and over and expecting a different result is the definition of ..."* well you know the rest of that quote. Sometimes we need to pause. We need to take a few steps in a different direction and come back to the task at hand. That momentary break gives us a fresh perspective, allowing us to see things differently.

A few years ago, we were training one of our Newfoundland dogs in water rescue. We were working on a particular exercise where Lilo (our dog) needed to swim out to "victims" stranded on a boat, carrying a rope in her mouth out to them. Each time I handed Lilo that rope, she bolted out into the water to "save" the people—but she'd drop the rope along the way. We worked on this exercise over and over. Each time, I set her up the same way, and each time she dropped the rope.

Training dogs is a challenging task for humans. When teaching a person how to do something—we can literally demonstrate the activity. But we can't demonstrate to the dog what we want him or her to do. We have to figure out a way to communicate so that the dog understands. This meant I had to change my technique— Lilo did not understand—and it was up to me to speak her language.

So we paused. We did other fun exercises. We moved in a new direction. And when we came back to that exercise—I had a fresh perspective; a new vision, new ideas, different technique … Lilo took that rope out to the boat! Lilo didn't need a refresh—I did! She clearly knew what to do—I just had to figure out how to tell her!

A refresh is a powerful tool. I have seen it work in training dogs, in handling a conversation, curing writers' block, learning a new sport—even finding the next step in one's career. Sometimes a literal "pause" is exactly what we need to realign our thoughts, our bodies—even our spirit—in order to move forward.

Don't be afraid to hit Refresh.

A momentary pause can lead you to amazing places!

3.11.16

# Timing!

"Timing is everything"...

"In the right place, at the right time"...

"Perfect timing"...

"When the stars and planets align"...

Is timing luck? Some certainly think so. We put a lot of emphasis on things happening at just the right time.  But what exactly is *the right time?"*

Everything that happens in our lives is a result of some other decision or event. Some call this the Butterfly Effect. They say when a butterfly flaps its wings on one side of the world; a wave is caused in an ocean on the other side of the world. The example is extreme but it basically means that in everything we do, with everyone we meet, a reaction is caused somewhere, somehow. Events and things that we may never know about transpire—all because of our actions.

- The clerk at your coffee shop is having money troubles. She's grumpy today but you smile at her. She smiles back— your smile changes her mood. The next customer remarks what great service he receives at this particular shop and gives her a big tip.
- You help your son catch the baseball each evening—he becomes pretty good. One night at practice, you watch your son help the new, shy kid on the team who has never played ball before. He and your son become best friends. Years later they both get baseball scholarships to college.
- You helped an employee many years ago learn to negotiate with a difficult client. Today that employee leads a successful global company—and is seen as a master negotiator.

Is timing coincidental? Do things just happen out of luck or magic? It may feel magical, but it's no accident. Timing is very deliberate and very powerful.

And it all starts with recognizing that everything we say, do and even feel—has an effect on the people and events in our lives today and long into the future.

Each time you flap your wings—a wave is created.

**Be the Butterfly!**

**The timing is always right!**

3.12.16

# Choice!

The older I become, or as I prefer to say, the more "ripened," I am amazed not only by the many choices we have in life—but the realization that those choices affect far more than we ever thought.

As kids, our lives were pretty much mapped out for us. Where we lived, what we studied, where we went to church, the sport we played—all were products of other people's decisions.

As adults we make decisions everyday. Some are large, some more trivial—but our days are often a series of very black and white decisions. We invest or we don't. We hire or we don't. We drink coffee or tea. Both conditions cannot exist at the same time.

Choice is something different. It's recognizing that many conditions exist at the same time—but it's where we choose to focus that is up to us. Choice is about perspective.

On a partly cloudy day, some will say: "Wow, look at all of the clouds." Others will say: "Look at that beautiful sun!" Both conditions are true. Both exist at the same time. Which one you focus on is your choice!

Last year, I resigned from my job and was looking for my next position. Shortly thereafter, my mother was diagnosed with cancer. And then one of our dogs got really sick. It was a pretty stressful time. But during this period—instead of focusing on the "blackness" that seemed to be in our lives—we chose to see something else. We saw a loving family—here for each other. We saw strength, courage and love. I was here with my family—exactly where I needed to be. We were taking this journey together. What a gift!

We all go through difficult situations. But rarely are they all black and white. There are shades of grey that add texture and dimension to every situation. It's up to us to see the grey!

**Every day you have a choice.**

**You can focus on the clouds or focus on the sun.**

**What do you choose to see today?**

3.13.16

# Thoughts!

We've all met someone that can't seem to catch a break. Ever wonder why? From money troubles, health issues, to broken cars—the list goes on. We all have difficult periods in our lives, but this friend, well her whole life is just a string of bad circumstances.

And when you speak to her, all she talks about are her troubles. Her posts on social media are negative no matter the subject— from politics to relationships. She believes life is unfair and her thoughts are consumed with how unlucky she is in life.

But is life just a product of circumstances and bad luck? Or do we actually play a role in creating or breaking things in our lives?

In order to fix something that is broken—you have to take it apart. You start with what you can see, and work backwards until you find the source of the problem.

Think of a leak in your home. You see a large puddle of water. Was it enough to just wipe up the water? Of course not. You can't just mop it up—you have to find where the water is coming from or else the water will destroy your home.

There is a drip of water coming down the wall. When you open the wall, you see more water; the pipes are really wet, but intact. You follow the pipe up the wall until you reach a joint. Water is now pouring out around the joint. When you take it apart—you see that the washer has gone bad.

You replace the washer and the leak stops. There is no more dripping and the water now flows freely through the pipes, just like it's supposed to.

We couldn't see the washer initially. The washer didn't appear to be doing anything—it wasn't loud or active in any way. And yet, that washer was capable of either creating a complete disaster or keeping things running smoothly.

Our thoughts are a lot like that washer. We can't see them—but they control how things flow in our lives. If you think you are unlucky, sick, broke, untalented … you start the leak. And the longer you think negatively—the larger the leak becomes, spilling out into all areas of your life.

Don't just mop up the water in your life.

Find the source of the leak and fix it!

It really is that simple.

Just like the washer … It all starts with our thoughts!

3.14.16

# Routine!

Wow—when one little thing changes in our daily routine, it can just throw off the entire day!

Yesterday was one of those days. Sunday was the first day of Daylight Savings Time. And if you're anything like me, this "springing forward" is really tough. I was thrown off all day—didn't know what time it was, didn't feel like dinner. I found myself still wide-awake at 1:30 this morning (and no, I am not typically a night owl)! Let's just say watching sporting clay training videos on You Tube until the wee hours of the morning did not make for a great start to my Monday!

Why does one little hour make such a difference? I mean really, it's only 60 minutes! Why? Because of routine. We become so engrained in our daily habits, we move throughout our day without any thought as to WHY we do some of the things that we do.

Doing something that becomes routine is not always a bad thing. Routine adds speed and fluidity to our actions. Just look at a well-run factory.

But there is a danger in routine as well. Driving a car is a pretty routine exercise for most of us. But have you ever arrived at work and didn't remember taking the last turn, or driving on a particular road? Routine …

With routine—we lose awareness. We act and respond so automatically that we forget WHY we are doing the things we do. And it is not until something is forced upon us, like a car swerving in front of us—or a time change—that we "wake up" from the routine.

But I have a plan! This year, I am choosing to spend the extra hours of sunlight in my day to do something new. Maybe an evening walk, or reading a book after dinner … It doesn't really matter what it is—the important thing is to do something different each day.

Do something, anything, to shake up the routine.

It's time to wake up!

3.15.16

# Kindness!

What exactly is kindness?

We read posts from friends on social media on a "pay it forward" campaign. In line at a drive-thru, he or she pays the bill for the person in the car behind. They post about their good deed and invite you to join in the crusade of doing these "acts of kindness." But is this really kindness? Charitable for sure—even generous. But maybe not "kindness."

A coworker of yours has a death in his or her family. You send food to the home and you attend the services. Is this kindness? Respect and support definitely (and maybe even a little obligation).  But still, not quite kindness.

What separates kindness from all of the other acts and virtues?

Ego.

The things we do often have a seed of benefit in it for ourselves. That's not necessarily a bad thing—but I'm not sure it's true kindness. When we act in a way that is 100% solely focused on the other person—well that is kindness. There is not a single thought of ourselves, what we get out of it, or even how it makes us feel.

There is no Ego.

When we look to nature—not all species have the capacity for charity or to show support. But almost all animals exhibit kindness.

Dogs typically do what is in their self-interest. They sit near you when they want attention. They bark to go outside or to be fed. They are not shy about putting their needs first.

And at the same time—we see kindness.

Several years ago we were at a dog show with our male Newfoundland, Iz. He was competing in obedience and a family was standing at the ring watching. They had a young boy with them in a wheel chair—he was severely affected, his head and arms were frozen in rather awkward positions. He was making noises, but could not speak. His mother wanted him to see Iz. Izzy was a young dog at the time—full of energy and really headstrong. He was 140 pounds and a real handful at a dog show. But as we walked up to the young boy, Iz became still, his energy changed. He sat himself quietly just under the young boy's hand. Izzy and the young boy sat there together for several minutes very peaceful and content—just sharing the moment.

I learned that day that kindness is an instinct. An instinct for dogs … and an instinct for humans.

Remove the Ego—follow your instinct.

That is kindness.

3.16.16

# Responsibility!

At what point does your responsibility end and another person's begins? This is a question we try to solve at work, at home—and in life.

How often do we hear someone say "I'll be happy when…"? That statement makes happiness a product of someone else's actions. Whether we intend to or not—conditions like these make our well-being someone else's responsibility.

That's not where we find happiness.

My husband and I watched a program on TV a few months ago about Spontaneous Order. This is a fancy term that basically means, when left alone—people, businesses, animals, markets—all naturally find order out of chaos by focusing on their individual efforts and activities.

They used an example of an ice skating rink. There is no one individual in the rink "in-charge" and establishing order. There is just one rule—everyone must skate counter-clockwise. There is no one making sure everyone skates at the same speed. There is no one limiting the style of skates, or the skill of the skaters. Each skater moves at a speed comfortable for him or her, and makes sure to steer clear of other skaters. Everyone settles into a natural rhythm, comfortably skating as individuals—and as a group.

I think life is like that skating rink. We can't wait for someone else to call the shots or set the rules. It's up to us to figure out what we want, and how fast we want to go.

When I was a little girl going to my first birthday party, I asked my mother, "What if I don't have a good time?" She said very calmly and gently "If you don't have a good time, it's no one's fault but your own."

Happiness is a personal responsibility.

I had a good time at that party.

3.17.16

# Quality!

More. We seem to always want more. From "all you can eat" buffets, "buy one get one free" sales, even my grocery store— "buy 10 pounds of cheese and get a free pound" (yes, the cheese is delicious but still) ...

But this kind of "more" focuses on number instead of substance. We become so preoccupied with "volume"—we no longer appreciate value.

I am an only child and fortunate to be very close to my parents. We're friends as well as family. I lived out of state for many years and during that time we had to travel to see one another. We couldn't just call up and go out to dinner at the spur of the moment. We didn't see each other a lot but when we did—it was always awesome. We were completely focused on one another, from meals to outings; we really made the most of our time together.

You see, because we were not able to get more in number, we focused on the quality of our time together. And there was "more"—we were more engaged, more present, more laughs ... More quality.

In business and in life—we are often seduced by "more." More employees, more friends, more cars, more toys, more shoes, more vacation days … it's all about quantity.

But something happens when you focus on Quality.

That is when you truly find … More!

3.18.16

# Plain!

A few weeks ago, I was in a dressing room trying on clothes at a department store. I had a minor scratch on my arm and didn't realize it had started to bleed. Yep, you guessed it—the blouse I was trying on was now covered in blood. I immediately told the sales associate I would buy the item.

Once home, I tried to find a solution for cleaning my new blouse. I posted to friends, I researched online. Certainly there was some new technologically advanced chemical solution that would take care of this stain. I was told to use everything from vinegar to compounds that I could not pronounce.

But a friend of mine suggested I use plain water. I was stunned—really? Just plain water! I placed the blouse under the tap—and within minutes—the stain was gone. A very plain solution solved a very big (and expensive) problem.

When you think about the most enjoyable days in your life—your mind probably remembers milestone events, major vacations, awards ceremonies … Big, splashy, spectacular occasions.

Now imagine a plain Saturday morning. You have nowhere you

need to be. You pour yourself a cup of coffee; the house is quiet except for your favorite music playing in the background. It's cool outside, but the sun is shining. You get comfortable in your favorite chair, and sit down to read the newspaper. Pretty soon two hours have passed.

How do you feel right now? Relaxed? Refreshed? Maybe even wanting a cup of coffee.

Somehow we allow life to get way too complicated. From projects at work, to whirlwind vacations—we assume that the more steps involved the better the result.

You'll probably never remember the "plain" moments in your life.

But just like breathing.

The simplest, most basic—is the most powerful.

3.19.16

# Tradition!

Yesterday was a pretty hectic day. I was out and about most of the day and evening. It was 9pm before I actually sat down. I put on the kettle and decided to enjoy a cup of tea.

But instead of using an everyday mug, I decided to enjoy my tea in a very traditional teacup and saucer. The cup is very old and belonged to my grandmother. For years, I kept this cup and saucer carefully put away in the china cabinet—I didn't want anything to happen to it. But in my sentimental reverence, out of fear really, I locked it away. And in doing so, I never used the cup, never looked at it—I actually never really thought about it.

A few months ago I was packing things up at our home, some to donate, others to reorganize—when I came across this cup and saucer. I was struck by how beautiful it was and I wondered—why don't I ever use this? What purpose does it serve hidden away?

How many of us have closets and drawers filled with things that we only take out for "special occasions?" Or maybe, like my teacup, they are so precious—we never take them out all?

I think life is our Special Occasion. It's meant to be lived and enjoyed right now—not someday in the future, and certainly not packed away out of fear.

Tradition is important.

We must remember it.

We must honor it.

We must learn from it.

We must experience it.

And ... we must live it.

I really enjoyed my tea.

Grandma would be pleased.

3.20.16

# Balance!

We are creatures that thrive in Balance. Just look at nature—it is based on balance. You can't have day without night. Flowers need rain and sun. Crops need rich soil and the proper temperature. Balance.

We are no different. Why then do we spend so much time focused on the extremes in our lives instead of the middle? Somehow we have associated balance with the boring or mundane. But I think it's in moments of balance where we rejuvenate and flourish.

I'm sure we've all worked with that person, when a problem arises—he or she explodes and lashes out at everyone else. You can almost feel the heat coming off of this person. We could even say he or she is "too hot."

There's no balance there.

Or how about that family member who brings everyone down? Every time you visit, he or she is negative about everything and gossips about other members of the family. You almost feel damp and chilly when you are together. We could say he or she is "too cold."

There's no balance there.

But balance finds us—whether we like it or not. That hothead coworker? Ends up having a heart attack. The negative family member? Becomes estranged from the family. Nature has a way of balancing everything ... even us.

I used to travel a lot. I kept a really intense schedule of 12+ hour days, back-to-back meetings and calls—there was A LOT of noise and activity in my days. One day I realized, each night back in my hotel room, I never turned on the TV. Now, this was pretty odd for me. At home, there is generally a TV on somewhere in our house. So why then did I never even think to turn it on in my hotel? Because I was naturally doing what my body needed— which was quiet and calm ... I was creating Balance.

Look at your life. Not at the extreme highs or lows, but at the moments where you feel peaceful, content, confident ...

That's the middle.

That's what Balance feels like.

Find the Balance ... everyday!

3.21.16

# Real!

Character. What is that? It is who we are at our core. It's what we stand for, believe in, how we live, feel—it's that something inside that makes us tick. Some could even call it—heart.

And in the moments when we listen to our heart and we follow our instincts—when we stay true to our character—that is when we are REAL.

The REAL you is always the BEST you. The person you are at home with your family. The person you are with lifelong friends. Is this the same person you are at the office, at church, on the team, in your organizations, at your kids' school?

We have become really good at compartmentalizing our lives and with it—ourselves. I think that's why there's so much focus on "work-life balance." We've created all of these different versions of ourselves that we yearn to just be … REAL.

I had the wonderful experience of going back to school to get my MBA in my mid-forties. I was surrounded by brilliant and accomplished people. It was an amazing and humbling experience. But I learned something besides the academics. I learned the importance of being REAL. It would have been easy for my classmates and I to put up walls, hide behind titles and experience—but we didn't. Instead we were honest and authentic. No compartmentalizing. No politicking. No pretense. And because of this—an amazing team was formed. A team based on trust. That is the power of being REAL.

To be successful, to feel fulfilled—you need to be REAL. You don't need to create different personas. Be honest. Be authentic. Be true to yourself. And if you find yourself in situations that go against your character—well that's not the right place for you.

Life is short. Work hard. Strive to be your best.

And your Best—is being REAL.

3.22.16

# Grateful!

What are you grateful for?

Typically when asked this question we respond with the big things like our family, friends, health ... But what about the things that haven't happened yet? Are you grateful for those too?

You should be.

In most sports, from golf to football, a coach asks a player "what's your plan?" He wants the athlete to visualize success in his mind and work backwards to figure out how to get there. The athlete sees victory *before* it even happens. And when it comes time to play, a funny thing occurs. The athlete's body naturally follows the mental picture he created. Success!

There are things we all worry about. There are things we hope to accomplish. But instead of hoping and worrying, why not be grateful? *Being grateful for something means we believe it will come to pass. It is a definite event in our lives.*

An athlete doesn't worry about the play—he visualizes victory! ***Being grateful is the first step in seeing victory in your*** *life.*

- Hoping to land a new, big account? Be thankful for the progress you have made so far and the benefit this new account will bring to you and your team.
- Waiting for a medical report? Be thankful you and your family support one another and you have excellent doctors who will bring you good news.
- Interviewing for a new job? Be thankful for the experience of meeting new people and the opportunity to make a difference in the lives of others.

Visualizing success isn't just for athletes. It's for everyone.

My husband always tells me "See your reality, be your reality."

He's right.

(Let's just not tell him ☺).

**What are you grateful for today?**

3.23.16

# Do!

"Do or do not. There is no try."

Insightful words from Yoda in Star Wars. But what does it really mean?

As a young child, I hated vegetables. I can remember my mom telling me "just try it." I had to at least attempt to eat one or two. I knew I didn't have to eat them all but she wanted me to at least make an effort. So I did the bare minimum.

As kids, many of us played sports or musical instruments. Our coaches and teachers again told us "just try." They expected us to take a first step, make an attempt, but had no expectation that we would be any good or we would succeed. And neither did we.

As professionals, we set goals. And we often tell the team "just try." In other words, don't worry about hitting the goal—just make an effort. We think the goal is a stretch anyway—and so do they. And no one hits the goal.

When we say we're going to "just try" we're basically saying—I know I probably won't succeed, but I'll at least do something.

This "just try" message, intended as a positive, ends up really doing a disservice. By thinking "just try" we are confirming our fears that we won't like it, won't be any good, won't hit the goal, can't succeed ... We are setting ourselves up to fail.

How negative. And what a defeatist attitude. Why should we allow ourselves to go through life sabotaging our own success?

If there is something you want to do—why not just decide to do it? Recognize that everything is a process. It may take practice, effort, determination, assistance ... But if there is something you want, don't let anyone stand in your way—especially yourself!

**Do or do not. There is no try.**

3.24.16

# Positive!

Ever wonder why, in the exact same situation, some people are negative while others are positive?

This is never more obvious than in an airport. Sitting in an airport recently, flights all around me were delayed due to weather in other parts of the country, causing a chain reaction.

The first gate announcement of an hour delay caused minor tatters and comments among some of the passengers. The second announcement of another hour delay led to some people pacing and waving arms while talking angrily on cell phones to ticket agents and colleagues.

But the fourth and fifth announcements with even longer delays—well that's when the true colors really emerged. People gasped, rolled their eyes—some even started venting to complete strangers sitting right next to them (not something you normally see in New York)! I heard one woman shout to anyone who would listen "Why do they keep doing this to us?"— as if it was personal.

Meanwhile, other passengers took advantage of the delay. One passenger was so engrossed in reading her book, she never even heard the gate announcements. Another, who had been on the go all day and almost missed his flight, now had time to grab dinner and relax a moment. And a father and son—they spent the time enjoying each other's company, playing a game together until the son fell asleep in his dad's lap.

How people react during situations out of their control is often how they react in all aspects of life.

Some become angry. Some gossip and vent. Some blame others. And some—make the most of any situation.

Being negative or being positive comes down to choice. We can't control what happens to us, but we can control how we view the situation, and more importantly, what we do about it.

Some choose to see the glass as half-full, others see a glass half-empty. And others make the most of the situation and drink the water!

The choice seems pretty obvious to me!

Cheers!

3.25.16

# Flow!

In my office at home I have a water fountain. It's a quiet, peaceful fountain. There's no sound from the pump or the motor, all you can hear is the sound of the water flowing.

In the top of the fountain, where the water pours out, there are a few rocks. I think they are meant to be decorative. No matter how many rocks I put in the top of the fountain, the water still finds a way to quietly flow.

Water is so peaceful and gentle. And yet, over time, this peaceful water will eventually erode the rock. And the hard, solid rock can never stop the water. There is no question which of the two has the true power.

We spend a lot of time trying to be like rock. We are rigid and sometimes even stubborn. We've been taught that being hard makes us more professional; being harsh and tough means we're strong. But is this really true? I don't think so.

I think it's better to be like water.

To live a life that is peaceful and calm. To move alongside

obstacles instead of fighting them.

To Flow ...

And yet always knowing, deep down inside ...

You have the power!

3.26.16

# Value!

It has been said, something is worth what someone else is willing to pay for it. We decide whether to buy something or invest in it when we perceive the value is equal to or greater than how much we are willing to pay for it.

At the grocery store, we may buy more chicken than we need when it is on special because we get more chicken for our money on that particular day. Or in business, we may buy merchandise in bulk because we get a better price per item, which means more value, when we purchase in large quantities.

But value goes beyond money. In the last year, I focused on my health and on eating better. I didn't go on a diet; rather I just established the "value" to me of the food I was eating. If it was "worth it"—I ate it. If it wasn't worth the calories I was investing— then I passed. I lost 40+ pounds and have kept it off following this investment philosophy.

But what about time? No matter how hard we work, or how fast we move throughout the day, most people feel like they just can't catch up. There just isn't enough time to get it all done.

Why? Because we don't "invest" time—we spend it. We react throughout the day to distractions, obligations, impulses ... even guilt. We spend our time on things that don't matter or aren't important—like worrying, gossiping or being negative. We do things that just deplete our time and don't add any value to our lives. That's not an investment—that's an expense.

There are those that can generate value from their money.

There are those that just spend it.

Time is no different.

No, you can't have more than 24 hours each day. But how you spend that time, and the value you produce with it for you and those around you—that is an investment decision.

And it all starts with one simple question ...

"Is it worth it?"

3.27.16

# Reflect!

Well the season has come to a close. Today is Easter, and spring has begun all over the country. And just like the flowers blooming and the birds chirping at my home—it really does feel like we have closed one chapter, and are beginning a new one.

I started this series at the beginning of Lent. As a child, I always gave up something—like chocolate or treats during this time. But at this stage in my life, I thought it would be more meaningful to spend some time focusing internally. To reflect …

This morning I went back and re-read each passage from the past 46 days. This season of reflection has had a profound effect on me. Sure, each day a thought or idea would come to me. I would write about something I saw in nature—or an event that had happened the day before.

But in reading the entire collection—I see a journey. A process of self-discovery that is a true gift and one in which I am very thankful.

I learned a lot during this time of Lent.

Jennifer Hansen

I learned that I am in control ... and yet I control nothing.

I learned that fear is unnecessary.

I learned that my attitude is a choice—not a result.

I learned that knowing who I am is the only opinion that matters.

I learned that if I empty my mind and open my heart—the answers come.

I learned that seasons change, not as an ending—but as a beginning.

I learned that nature is a valuable teacher—I just need to listen.

I learned that sometimes it _is_ about Faith.

I learned that by doing what is right—always leads to what is good.

And most of all—I've learned the power of reflection. To take time to be still. To be empty. To be open. To think. To feel. To be.

This is not "The End" of the story. But this chapter is "Complete."

It's time to turn the page ...

# Butterfly ...

Jennifer Hansen

4.22.16

# Does Faith Belong in Business?

The title is somewhat controversial. You probably assumed this article would be about the intersection of religion and the workplace. Well, you would be wrong. Faith is certainly part of many religions—but Faith is more than that. To me, Faith is a belief. It's about conviction. **It's about … knowing.**

Like many of you—I like to be in control. Not in a "control-freak" sort of way—but there is a sense of comfort in predictability. I plan my day and feel good when I accomplish the things I set out to do. I like to be on time for meetings and appreciate when others are too. And I love when deals close and events happen just as I thought they would.

People who have worked with me have heard me say many times "Hope is not a strategy!" And I think this is true. It takes work, research, planning and most of all—bringing the right people together—to create a successful strategy. You can't just passively "hope" that everything will magically happen.

So where does Faith come in? There comes a moment when all the planning, and the work comes together—the strategy is complete. Then what? Then you have Faith. You believe, actually—you just KNOW—whatever happens next is what is supposed to happen.

Think of an artist—at some point the paint is on the canvas and he stops. Does the paint dry exactly as the artist envisioned? No. Does it look like what he first imagined before he even picked up a brush? Probably not. It changed and developed in many ways throughout the process. But in that moment, the artist believes, he feels ... he just *knows* ... it is finished—and it is good.

Faith.

I'm not saying everything happens exactly like we expect it to all of the time. But Faith is believing, whatever does happen—you are prepared and equipped to handle it. It's a feeling that as events unfold, they will eventually lead to something even better than you imagined.

**Faith is knowing whatever the outcome—it is good.**

4.26.16

# F-A-I-L ... Is not a Four-Letter Word!

All of my life, I have strived to not just succeed—but to excel. To do more and be better than what others expected. I had good grades, did well in school—I even graduated with my Bachelors degree in 2 ½ years while working a full time job. Whatever I put my mind to—I just did it.

In my 20's I believed the goal was perfection and nothing less was acceptable. Some people fear clowns, others spiders—well for me it was failure. That "nasty word" did not exist in my vocabulary ... and it certainly was never an option.

What I didn't realize back then—is that I was failing. By only focusing on perfect results—I wasn't allowing myself the opportunity to grow and to learn. Because it's when things don't go as planned, when we stumble or make mistakes—that is when we truly learn.

I heard someone say that if you don't ever fail—it means you aren't trying new things. You're not stretching and challenging yourself. I think this is true.

Today, in my 40's I feel differently about this word. I've certainly had my share of failures, and I've also had a lot of successes—both personally and professionally. But you know what's funny? The things I take the most pride in are not the big splashy accomplishments listed on a resume. Rather, it's the small personal moments when I made a mistake or things didn't go as planned—and I took the opportunity to learn. When success didn't just accidentally happen—but was a result of my efforts to discover a better solution. The times I challenged myself to think differently, to try new things—to go beyond my comfort zone. Those are the milestones that truly matter to me.

I still get a pit in my stomach when I realize I've made a mistake—especially if it means I've hurt another person or let someone down. But I don't ever want that feeling to go away. Because that feeling is like a voice whispering in my ear saying: "This is an opportunity...*SEIZE it!*"

5.4.16

# Beauty and Strength!

I love lilies—they are my favorite flower. And I especially like Lilly of the Valley. My great grandmother grew them, so I guess they always remind me of her. They are small and delicate and have a sweet, yet distinct scent. The flowers hang from what seems to be a small thread, and they look as if any amount of wind would blow the blooms right off of the stem. So delicate—they must need tender loving care to bloom. Ahh—so wrong!

Beauty and Strength! We often think of these two things as separate and opposite. If something is "beautiful," it's perceived as delicate, weak—maybe even out of reach. And something that is strong—well, it's thought to be hard, cold and inflexible.

And yet, nature proves us wrong. It teaches us balance.

When I think of the most beautiful things in nature—the ocean, a tall pine tree, even my Lilly of the Valley—each is flexible, each is adaptable, they are all beautiful—and all VERY strong. They are not just one characteristic or the other. In fact, it is the simultaneous balance of beauty and strength that makes them awesome.

I believe we are at our best when we balance "beauty and strength"—when we are calm yet confident, flexible yet determined, curious yet decisive, compassionate yet tough ...

The Lilly of the Valley doesn't let anything stand in its way. One of the lilies bloomed from within the asphalt of our driveway. It looked like it was growing on the surface of the moon. It pushed through amazing obstacles to reach its goal—**and it bloomed. With Beauty ... and Strength!**

5.28.16

# Focus on the Moment!

We have the opportunity to learn even from the most ordinary teachers. Like eggs …

I am a morning person. I wake up ready to tackle the day. At one time, it was not unusual for me to start a load of laundry, answer emails and read a report from work—all while eating breakfast. I couldn't tell you what I actually ate for breakfast, it was just one more thing I was doing—something to check off the list.

Down the road from our home is a little farm. On the roadside, they have a cart set up where they sell, on the honor system, homemade baked goods, fresh seasonal produce—and eggs. Fresh eggs from free-range chickens, with bright orange yolks. I love eggs.

About a year ago, I committed to myself to live a healthier lifestyle. To eat better and to exercise. And today, one year later, I feel great. But it's not just the weight I've lost, or the energy I found—it's the lessons I learned along the way that made the biggest impact.

I love soft-boiled eggs. And of all the ways to make eggs—this to me is the hardest. The eggs need to be at room temperature before you put them in a soft boil, where they are precisely timed for five minutes. The toast needs to be ready at the exact moment the eggs are finished or the eggs will keep cooking while you wait for the toast. It's like a dance—and takes complete focus.

I found in my new healthy lifestyle, I needed protein in the morning and what better source of protein than eggs a few mornings a week? I was determined to cook them soft-boiled. Some mornings they were runny, other mornings they were hard. I learned I needed to pay attention, to be completely in the moment, and focus on one thing—my breakfast—to get those eggs just right.

Look around. Our lives are filled with work, soccer games, board meetings, vacations—often all at the same time! We try to jam as much as possible into every minute of the day. And when we are supposed to be doing one thing, like watching our child score during the soccer game, we're checking email and posting on social media. We focus on so many things—that we see nothing.

My husband is a photographer. He has taught me that you don't just take a picture of a broad landscape with lots of trees and wildlife—there will just be too much going on in the photo—too many distractions. Rather, you focus on one element in that landscape: a tree, a bird, a flower—that's what gives the picture interest, depth, and feeling.

Focus. Be in the moment … All in.

I made my eggs this morning. They were perfect!

Jennifer Hansen

## 5.31.16

# Balanced Relationships ...

Several years ago, my then boyfriend and I were visiting an island in the Great Lakes and we rented a bicycle for two. I was sitting on the front seat—my boyfriend had the rear seat. The island was a little hilly, and when we got to one of the hills, I stopped pedaling—leaving my boyfriend to do all of the work. Throughout our day I would periodically stop pedaling and he would complain that this was a lot of work—he wasn't aware that I had stopped pedaling! I laughed when he discovered my trick. I had a great time! My boyfriend said he would never ride a tandem bike with me again!

I think relationships are a lot like that bicycle. Whether at home with our families, or at work with our colleagues—there is give and take. At different times, some people are able to give more; others can only give so much. But it's the commitment to one another that ensures the combined effort equals 100%.

We've heard it said that relationships are 50/50. Well, I don't think that's true. I think relationships, whether personal or professional—are just 100%. Sometimes they're a combination of 50/50, other times 40/60, sometimes even 99/1. But it's the combined effort that totals 100%.

But that's just in the short-term. To make sure the results are repeatable and long lasting—you need balance. Just like that bicycle, it was certainly possible for us to get around the island with just my boyfriend pedaling. But was it sustainable? How long could we survive with only half of the team pulling 100% of the weight?

Things can be out of balance for a time. There are times we need to coast. And times we are the ones pedaling.

But just like that bicycle—the only way to keep moving forward—is with balance.

Balanced vision. Balanced strategy. Balanced direction. Balanced effort. Balanced momentum. Balanced energy. Balanced relationships.

Balance ...

8.10.16

# Thermometer or Thermostat?

The other day I was listening to Joel Osteen on the radio and I heard him ask this question: "Are you a Thermometer or a Thermostat?" Maybe because we are having one of those REALLY hot and humid Mid-western summers, when I heard this question—it really got me thinking.

A thermometer is a gauge. It informs. And let's face it—the only time we really use a thermometer is when conditions are negative. An illness, a hot August day, a frigid night in February, or even to monitor sensitive equipment—*a thermometer gives us information regarding a potentially negative situation.*

But a thermostat—well that's something entirely different. Yes, it may have a temperature gauge on it but a thermostat is a TOOL—it actually DOES something. It Acts. It evaluates conditions and then performs a task to improve the situation. Its sole purpose is to act in such a way that it improves the environment ... It creates change. *Thermostats are all about MAKING things positive.*

We're all "thermometers" at times. We get home at night and complain about the rush hour traffic. But did talking about it improve the drive or make our evening at home more enjoyable? No. At work, we complain about a coworker who dropped the ball again. But did gossiping to others help that employee become better? Not at all.

We all know people that thrive on being thermometers. They talk about spouses, coworkers, the weather, even the presidential race. They feel it is their duty to inform you of the latest negative news happening in their family, at the office, in politics—in his or her life.

Before you share the next story, problem or bit of news with someone, ask yourself—does this help? Will I improve the environment with this story? Am I making the situation better for my friend? For myself? Does talking about this subject help me to find a solution? *Am I highlighting the negative—or am I MAKING things positive!*

It's important to communicate, discuss and even debate with one another. *But the true goal of any exchange—is positive impact. To* learn, to gain understanding, to improve a situation ... to be of service to others and to ourselves—that's impact. Our words, our actions—all focused on improving the environment.

Report the news or make the news!

Wallow in the problems or bask in the solutions!

Talk about it or BE about it.

Jennifer Hansen

Thermometer or Thermostat ... Which are you?

It really is a choice!

8.14.16

# Who do You Want in Your Lifeboat?

Imagine—you're on a ship that suddenly has mechanical problems. You and the other passengers must evacuate. You're captain of a lifeboat and must choose who goes in your boat. You have written profiles on each passenger, and you get five minutes with your "candidates" to determine who joins your boat. You read from the profiles that some of the passengers have been rescued in lifeboats before. Who do you choose?

The easy answer is to choose all of the passengers with prior "lifeboat experience." Surely they *must* know exactly what to do. But do they? They know where the life jackets are stored, they even know what the equipment is called, but does that mean they can help you and the rest of the team survive? This may be the easy answer—but it clearly may be the wrong one.

Think about business. This scenario is not that different from hiring. Each time we add a new person to our team, we are bringing someone "onto the lifeboat." Is this the time to take the easy way out? Of course not. Then why do so many make the "safe" decision and hire based on experience? Why do we assume that if the candidate knows our industry's language, the names of the key players, or even our product—that makes him or her the best person for our team?

Why? Because of fear. Hiring is a great big unknown. We don't want to make a mistake and are looking for a sure thing. **But sure things are not found in experience.**

Let's go back to our lifeboat example. What you really want to know—is the candidate *a good problem solver*? Can he or she *make good, sound timely decisions*? Will he or she *act in the face of uncertainty*? Will he or she *fit with the other members of the team?*

Over the years I have had the pleasure of hiring hundreds of professionals. Some of my best hires were candidates that came from outside our industry. No, they didn't know the lingo or the competitive landscape (but that was quickly and easily taught). They were successful because they were problem solvers. They were smart. They could make decisions. And most of all—they were the right fit with the team.

Conversely over the years, some of my most unfortunate hiring decisions were candidates with lots of direct industry experience. Perhaps I had unfair assumptions that he or she wouldn't need a learning curve. Perhaps I assumed "he must be good, he's done it." But each time I made the "easy decision," the one that felt "safe"—it ended up being disastrous for the team—and for me.

Leading many companies, are CEOs that seamlessly moved from one industry to another. From consumer products to technology; from automotive to entertainment; from beer to hospitality; these

CEOs were not hired because they were industry experts. **They were chosen because they are problem solvers ... because they are leaders.**

As you fill your lifeboat, you need shipmates that can weather the waters ahead, not relive the journeys of the past. You have a choice—hire an *"Anchor"*—someone that knows where the life jackets and oars are kept, and will keep you tied in place, safe and secure—but moving nowhere.

Or hire a *"Rudder"*—someone that moves you forward by utilizing the oars as a new mast, adapting the life jackets into a great sail, and catches the wind—transforming your lifeboat into a great sailing vessel.

**Who do you want in your lifeboat?**

8.21.16

# Leading Through Change!

Some people go to a gym. Others run. I walk. I like to walk in a park near my home and when I feel particularly energized, I take the outer loop—the "hilly loop." It's three miles of pretty steep hills and valleys. Towards the end of this trail, the path emerges from the woods at the top of a hill and I'm staring down a long, deep valley. And on the other side of this valley? You guessed it—another REALLY big hill. Not just any hill, but a *"Why am I doing this?"* kinda hill!

I have come to hate this valley. Why? Because I know "THAT hill" is just on the other side of it. It's going to be tough. It's not going to feel good and I'll wonder why I'm putting myself through this.

But today when I got to that usual spot, for some reason instead of looking down in the valley, I looked out ahead. And then I saw it. Beyond the valley, and beyond "THAT hill," I saw an amazing view. And I realized what I was looking at in the distance was exactly where my trail ends. Each time that I have walked this trail, I was so focused on that valley, fearing "THAT hill" ahead, I had no idea my journey took me to somewhere so beautiful.

Change is a lot like that trail. We all walk through valleys where we fear the road ahead. There are times where we are facing "THAT hill" and we wonder, "Why am I doing this?" But maybe, just maybe if we knew what the outcome would be like, if we could see ahead beyond the valleys and the hills—well suddenly it all starts to make sense … and it all feels worth it.

As leaders, we have the responsibility (and the privilege) to help those around us get through these periods. Whether it's times of reorganization, new management, product launches or failures—there are times that are unknown, uncertain and uncomfortable.

It's important to communicate about those valleys and hills—A LOT.

But ask yourself—have you painted a clear picture of the final destination for your team? Does everyone understand where we are going? What life will be like once we get there? Why are we doing this? How will we get it done? And most of all—what will this do for the company, the customers, the shareholders, and the employees?

We've all witnessed amazing moments during the Olympics. I don't claim to be an athlete, but I've heard many coaches say—in order to win, you have to visualize winning. You can't just focus on running the race, or the next lap. You have to actually SEE the finish line in your mind and you winning. You need to know, feel, see and understand the final destination … and then do it.

We can't take away the valleys or the hills. But we can make sure everyone sees the view ahead. It might just be pretty amazing!

8.31.16

## "I am Still Learning..." —*Michelangelo Age 87*
## ARE YOU?

Over the past few weeks, my social media newsfeeds have been filled with photos of my friends' children all heading back to school. New clothes, new backpacks, and bright smiling faces— it's as if these photos are saying "ready, set ... Learn!"

Ask yourself—**when is the last time you learned something new?** Anything. Can you name it? Do you remember where, when or even why? Probably not.

I often hear colleagues say—"boy, I really liked school. I miss that time." Or "I wish I liked to read more, it's just not my thing." Or "work is so stressful, I just need to escape when I read or go to the movies."

At some point as adults, we figured out that being *comfortable* was a lot better than being *uncomfortable*. And we naturally seek out situations where we feel ... *comfortable;* restaurants where we know we like the food, friends that think just like we do, and yes even our careers. We put ourselves in situations that feel good, feel familiar—where we are confident we have all the answers.

But in doing so, we lose something—learning. Because let's face it—learning is uncomfortable. It means encountering things we don't know how to do, don't understand or worse yet—don't have the answers. And it feels, you guessed it—*uncomfortable*.

Deep down, there is a certain comfort in having all of the answers—I like to call this *"expert mode."* It's that feeling at work or even in our personal lives, where we believe we know it all. That pretty much, any situation that comes our way—we will have the answer. And that feels good. So we stay there—and we stop learning.

But living in "expert mode" is dangerous. At some point, something is going to challenge us. We are going to be rocked by a situation where we don't have the answers: a sickness, a financial setback, an unanticipated product failure. And because we stopped seeking out new ways of thinking or doing—not only will we not have the answer—we won't know how to find it.

Learning isn't defined by a particular time period in our lives. It's not about elementary school or college. After all, I would hate to think all there is to learn in life happens between the ages of 5 and 22. What about the other 60+ years after that?

I believe the more advanced we become in our careers, the more important it is to keep learning. This doesn't mean we read fancy textbooks or take complicated courses—although those are both great. Learning is about change. It's about thinking differently. Instead of seeking only comfortable situations—it's embracing the *uncomfortable* and seeing it as an opportunity to grow and to learn.

There are many successful CEOs that move from industry to industry—from airlines to automotive, entertainment to consumer products. Are these individuals "experts" on every industry? Of course not. But they each have one thing in common.

They are problem solvers.

Why? Because they continue to learn. They continue to challenge themselves. They understand they are not "experts" but rather students—and they strive to better understand the world and themselves everyday.

*When is the last time you learned something new?*

*Why not today!*

9.15.16

# How Much do We Really Control?

I am a driven person. Many of us are. And when there is an outcome I feel strongly about—I put forth _a lot_ of effort to ensure it happens. And over time, the more successful we become, and the more those outcomes actually materialize—we convince ourselves we have the ability, the power—to "control" the outcome.

Until we realize ... we don't.

As a young professional, I thought my job was to ensure perfection. I worked hard to make sure there were never any mistakes. And the more advanced I became in my career, and the more things there were to manage—the more things that could go wrong. So I did what I always did—I just worked harder and harder to ensure perfection—to make sure ALL desired outcomes (mine, my bosses', my employees', my customers', my family's)— all outcomes were achieved.

But is that sustainable? Is it even realistic? Of course not. Let's face it—sometimes things are in conflict. A customer wants one price and your business needs another. Your spouse wants a vacation and you have a conference that same week. You ship the products on time, and they are delayed due to a snowstorm.

I've written a lot about the many lessons I've learned in the simple moments of life. Several mornings a week, I make myself eggs. Most mornings—I enjoy delicious eggs. But sometimes, just after I put the eggs in the water—the shells crack. Why? I didn't miss a step. I did everything the same as the day before.

Because we can't control everything. Maybe the eggs were bigger or smaller? Maybe the shells were thinner? Maybe the water was slightly too hot, or the eggs still too cold? There are ALWAYS other factors that we just don't know, can't see and definitely—cannot control.

Now many years later—I am still driven. I strive for ambitious goals. But the path I take has changed. I have learned success is not defined by perfection. It is not the absence of mistakes nor is it just one outcome. Success is a process and when we let go, and are open—the possibilities before us become bigger and better than we ever imagined.

I can't control every situation. I can't "will" every outcome into reality.

But what can I control?

My decision to move on or keep going. My willingness to learn. My ability to adapt. My response. My attitude.

Me …

9.21.16

# Is Your Organization Really DIVERSE?

Diversity. It has become a noun, an adjective—even a verb. In the past few years there has been heightened focus across many industries and organizations to "diversify." Annual business plans, even compensation packages for business executives, are often tied to a goal of "diversification"—involving race, gender, even ethnicity.

I am not here to comment about the merits of such a system or philosophy. But I think there is an even greater area of "diversity" that we are missing—**the diversity of thought.**

We all have biases. But the one bias that is seldom talked about is *industry-bias*. Look across your organization. Your employees may look different; speak varying languages—but how many members of the team have spent their careers in your industry? I bet the majority. And yes, they are successful. They have great connections, and deep product knowledge.

But what is missing?

When was the last time someone on your team had a breakout idea? I don't mean the everyday ideas coming from the strategy or product development folks—it's their job to have ideas. *I mean a "business-changing" idea.* Is anyone suggesting a new way to go to market? A new process for accounting? How about a way to streamline inventory?

We assume what bonds our teams together is the industry. That the common denominator to their success is this unwritten, "secret handshake" that they all must know because they've paid their dues and earned their stripes working in the same industry. We convince ourselves that our industry is unique—that the nuances, the challenges, the language, the "keys to success" are so specific to our industry—they can only be understood, and more importantly—achieved, by those working within that industry.

But that couldn't be further from the truth.

What makes a good team great? What takes a business from mediocre to exceptional? I think it comes down to three things: **Courage. Trust. Insight.**

**Courage**—to stop doing things that aren't working. And **Courage** to change and to try new things.

**Trust**—shared between employees, management, customers, shareholders … A **Trust** that everyone is committed to the best interests of each other and to the best interest of the business.

**Insight**—an *honest* understanding of the current state of the business and of the market. And more importantly, a thirst to continue to learn, grow and evolve. To not merely react to the future—but to shape it—for the company and the industry.

When we put so much emphasis on building our teams solely from within our industry, we forget what is really important—to bring together a group of qualified people, *possessing different but complimenting skills,* who when working together—produce amazing results.

Sure, there are some roles where we may need very specific industry experience. I don't want a dentist performing heart surgery—no matter how talented the dentist. But ask yourself, just how critical is industry experience?

Relying on industry experience feels safe. Sure, the learning curve may be shorter, but what are we talking about here—a couple of months? There may be a short-term payoff but there is definitely a very real long-term risk.

When we make repeated hiring decisions based on industry experience, over time, our organizations become homogenous. We end up doing things the same way year after year.

We begin to believe that status quo is good enough. We become reactive instead of proactive. Our competition surpasses us. And we are ripe for disruption or even take-over.

Why?

Because we got comfortable. Because we stopped challenging

ourselves to think differently. Because we forgot how the business started—by people with varying skills, perspectives and ideas. Because we built an organization where everyone thinks the same.

In my mid-forties I made the decision to go back to school to get my MBA. I learned many things throughout this experience. But the most important—that all business, no matter the industry, is the same. It's about people. It's about process. It's about product. And if you understand all three—you can be successful.

The program I selected was geared toward mid and senior level executives. Throughout our 20 months together, we worked in teams on MANY complex projects. These projects required us to quickly become "industry experts" across many industries and to solve some pretty significant problems for real businesses. It was not unusual that on one team there would be someone from pharmaceuticals, defense, consumer goods, technology, finance, or even entertainment.

And each time—an amazing thing happened. These teams of high-performing, industry-diverse, smart individuals, not only quickly adapted and learned the specifics surrounding the project—they asked questions and brought a fresh perspective to the problem. It was BECAUSE of their unique industry experience, that they uncovered solutions that were game changing to these businesses.

As business leaders, our job is to manage the short-term and lead for the long term. And how do we do that? Well, it's not by playing it safe. It's not by staying comfortable. It's not by hiring people that all think alike.

It's through Courage. It's through Trust. It's through Insight. And it's through Diversity ... Diversity of thought!

10.3.16

# Who are You?

What is the most important quality of a leader? Ask this question in any business school and you will receive many different answers. Some will focus on specific skills—like business acumen, financial aptitude or technical expertise. Others will speak of personality traits like integrity, tenacity or courage.

And yes, in many ways—these answers are all right. Good leaders are and possess many of these things. But I believe there is one— one single quality that a leader MUST possess that guides everything else.

Self-Awareness.

Leadership is a lot like coaching a football team. The coach knows which players compliment each other—and which don't work well together. He knows which teams they should defeat and which will be a challenge. He understands which plays his team can run and which they can't. He even understands how the environment—the weather, a different stadium—all affect the performance of his team.

But those are the _technical_ aspects of the game. The _external_ elements the coach must consider.

But the best coach understands something else—Himself.

What kind of coach am I? *What's important to me* in my players and in the game? *What do I value* and what won't I tolerate? *What is a "non-negotiable"* for me both on and off the field? Which players have I let down in the past? *How do I avoid that again?* How am I able to bring out the best in these players? *How do I repeat that* season after season?

As leaders—we focus on the product we produce, the process we use and the people that work for us. We even consider ourselves "experts" in many of these areas.

But there is one important element that we seldom focus on— ourselves. Just like the coach of a football team—*our words, our actions, even our very energy—have a profound impact on the business.*

I once witnessed a group of people at a company. While working for one boss, they performed adequately. And yet for another boss, this same group of people exceeded all expectations. What changed? You might think—the second boss was more skilled. He had a better strategy, hired better people or even changed the product offering. And yes, that might be true.

But at the heart of the change—the second boss knew himself. He knew his own strengths, and his own weaknesses. He knew how to build a team, produce a product and drive business—not

DESPITE himself—but because of himself. He understood that through his influence, his coaching, his words—even his specific energy—the team would not just perform—they would succeed.

How many times have we seen a football team get a new coach and suddenly the team starts winning? Did the rules of the game change? Of course not. Did this coach suddenly invent some miraculous new plays? Doubtful. Did the coach fire the entire team and suddenly draft new players—NO!

The difference was what this new coach brought to the game. The energy, the influence, and the talent he was able to elicit from these very same players. How was this coach able to do this? Because he knew himself. *He understood his role with this specific team, in this specific game, even on this specific day.*

*Just as our skills evolve over time—so do our hearts.* What we value, what motivates us, even the type of people we want to surround ourselves with—all changes over time. Knowing yourself as a leader is not just about knowing WHAT you are good at or not—it's about knowing WHO you are.

Take some time and get to know yourself.

You may know WHAT you are good at but have you ever asked yourself—WHY? Really ask yourself. It's in those answers that you will meet someone pretty awesome.

YOU!

10.9.16

# Seasons ...

What a beautiful fall morning. I currently live in the Midwest—the leaves are turning, it's 45 degrees this morning, and a flock of geese just flew overhead beginning their journey south. It is definitely fall.

When I think about the seasons, I know many people who say, "I hate summer—I can't take the heat or humidity." Or others claim, "winter is awful, it's so depressing and cold." And yet I have never, <u>and I mean NEVER,</u> met someone who doesn't like fall. Across the East, there are cruises, tours, festivals ... millions of people flock to enjoy and experience this glorious season.

But what is fall really? **Change!** Fall is nothing more than one season ending and transitioning into something new. In fact—it's the epitome of change! And it's the change itself which we find so beautiful!!!

So why then do people LOVE this kind of change and yet, in all other areas of life—they struggle with change? New jobs, reorganizations, layoffs, new hires, new homes, and new schools—anytime we have an event in our lives that is filled with change—we are filled with dread. WHY?

I don't think it's really the "change" that we hate. I think what we are really experiencing is fear. Fear of the unknown.

Consider this—if you REALLY hated change, would you ever take a vacation—go somewhere you have never been to experience something you have never seen or done? No! If you *truly* hated change, you would just stay home. And yet, we plan trips and spend money to visit places we have never been, to get away and experience something new. In fact, we look forward to this—we don't dread it! What's the difference?

Because we are not afraid. We have done our research, talked to friends and we trust we will enjoy ourselves. There is no fear! *Just excitement, curiosity, and confidence that no matter what happens—we will not only handle it—we will have a great time.*

There are times we guide others through change. Our employees, our children, family members or friends. From little moments to big life-altering events—we lead others through these periods. How do we make it easy?

By being honest. By being compassionate. By communicating.

And then there are times—WE are faced with change. Let's embrace it just like that vacation. With the confidence that no matter what happens—we can handle it.

We will learn from it. And we will be richer for the experience!

I just love fall …

10.26.16

# Lessons from my Dog ...

Over the past 11 years—My husband and I had the honor and the privilege to own Iz— our first Newfoundland dog. Since that time, we have brought other dogs into "our pack"—but Iz was our first—and he taught me a lot.

When Iz was just a puppy—I remember his first bath. When we were finished he experienced the blow dryer for the first time— and he was scared. He stood up on his hind legs and wrapped his "not so little" paws around my neck. He seemed to say "Save me Mommy"... and my heart melted. I scooped him up and babied him. And in doing so—I rewarded his fear. The next time we tried to dry him—he squirmed and acted afraid.

I realized—I needed to show him confidence. He needed to understand if I was not afraid—he didn't need to be afraid.

*I learned—reward the behavior I want repeated.*

When Izzy was an adolescent—he had a lot of energy. At night he would suddenly run at top speed from room to room, leaving a wake of destruction in his path—from dumped glasses on coffee tables to stolen shoes. I would try to catch him, at first calmly calling his name, escalating to screaming at him as I ran after him. And the louder I yelled—the faster and more mischievous he became.

One time—not knowing what else to do—my husband and I just stood up and turned our backs to him. We were completely silent. Izzy stopped and looked at us. We stood there for a long time and Iz quietly came and sat next to us.

*I learned—a quiet energy can have a strong affect.*

When Izzy was an adult—we did everything with him. From competing in conformation dog shows to training in water rescue. He was a large, beautiful intact male weighing in at 145 pounds. That was A LOT of dog to walk around—especially among lots of other dogs. One time at a dog show, I was attempting to walk Iz through the vendor booths—but he was really walking me. He nearly pulled me down to the ground!

A long-time breeder approached me, fixed Izzy's collar and walked him forward like he meant business. Izzy just got in line and walked along comfortably and calmly. I remembered something that our trainer once told me: "dogs will either lead or follow—there is nothing in between." I realized Izzy was just trying to find his place.

*I learned—if I want someone to follow—I need to lead.*

In the last year, Izzy had a few medical conditions. Some were mild annoyances for him, others were serious and required our diligent attention for his survival. Because of one of these conditions, we hand-fed Izzy his meals and he had to sit upright afterwards for fifteen minutes. In the beginning, I would try to do other things while Izzy was sitting. I would fold laundry or clean up the kitchen. And each time, Izzy would try to lie down. So then I would stand next to Izzy, but I would check my email or look at the Internet. And each time, Izzy would bark at me. But if I sat with Iz—and talked to him, played a game with him, or just looked into his eyes petting him—well then he would sit for the full 15 minutes.

I realized he needed my focus. He needed my presence. He needed me.

*I learned—being in the moment, being fully present—is a gift ... but it's not a gift we give. It's a gift we receive!*

We said goodbye to Izzy last week.

Many people will say that it's the human that teaches the dog.

I know that's not true. Izzy already had all of the answers. I just needed to listen.

Thank you Izzy.

**You taught me well.**

**I am a better human because of you.**

11.18.16

# Listen to Your Gut!

We make decisions everyday. Some are automatic—like what to have for breakfast. Some are quick—like what to wear to the meeting. And other decisions feel monumental—like whom to hire for the new position or what new product to launch.

We put a lot of pressure on ourselves to get these "big" decisions right. And yet, we don't give a thought to the hundreds of "small" decisions we make throughout the day. We just make them and move on. Why? Because we trust ourselves. Because we listen to our gut. Because we know we will make the right decision. And if the outcome is different than expected—we trust we will correct it quickly and appropriately.

You may be thinking—"Ah but Jennifer, some of those decisions are pretty low risk. Eating eggs instead of toast for breakfast, or wearing the blue suit instead of the red one doesn't really change anything does it?"

Well, what if the eggs have gone bad and you are sick all morning and miss an important meeting? Or what if red is the company color where you are interviewing today and you make a great impression? I would say both of those decisions could lead to some pretty "big" outcomes—even though they seemed like "small" decisions.

So then why don't we have the same faith in ourselves regardless of the magnitude of the decision? Because of fear. We don't want to make a mistake. And making a mistake means failure.

When faced with "big" decisions—of course we need to do our homework. Let's take hiring for example—selecting the right person to be part of a team is not an exact science. There are many variables to consider. Who is currently on the team and what does the team need from this new hire? How is the company changing and what type of person will we need, not just for today—but next year, five years from now? What is changing in the industry and what does the company need in order to be better prepared for the future?

But after you ask yourself all of these questions; after you have interviewed all of your candidates; and after you have sought the advice of your colleagues and employees—there is one step left. The most important step.

Listen to your gut.

There comes a point when your head and your heart become aligned. When you just "feel it." When you know.

When I think back to the hundreds of people I have hired in my career, there are a few that stand out to me. Some were disasters, where I hired only for experience or industry connections—and thought only with my head—and ended up neglecting the fit with the team.

Or another decision where I thought only with my heart—and hired the candidate everyone liked but wasn't actually suited to do the job—and ended up frustrating everyone on the team.

But my best hires? The ones that were wildly successful for the business, for the employee, and for me? Those were when my head and my heart said to each other—*"This is the one."*

It was when I listened to my gut.

It wasn't necessarily about experience. It wasn't generally about connections. It wasn't even about education. It was always because of Character. It was always because of Fit. It was always because—I just knew …

I knew I was making the right decision.

And if circumstances would change, and for some reason in the future, this might not play out as I expected, I also knew—I would make the right decision then too.

That's how it works when you listen to your gut.

You know you have what it takes to make the right decision for every situation.

It's not about failure.

It's not even about success.

It's about listening.

It's about <u>trusting</u> yourself.

It's about knowing who you are!

12.14.16

# Letting Go ...

My husband taught me a valuable lesson.

He told me to make a fist.

And then he asked, "Can you hold anything with that closed fist?"

Of course I could not.

Then he told me to open my hand.

And then he asked, "Now can you fill your hands?"

Of course I could.

In life we hold onto ideas, places, things and even people so tightly—that in the holding on—we prevent ourselves from grasping, reaching and even being filled with something new.

I grew up thinking my life would be a certain way. I would go to school, have a nice job, get married, have children—even live in a certain location.

And in clinging to those ideas, holding on to those visions—I was closing my fist.

You see that was not my path—it never was. My journey takes me somewhere different—to do things I haven't even thought of yet.

Over the past two years I have learned a lot. Most of which you have read in these previous pages. I learned about Balance. Failure. Fear. Strength. Self-Awareness. And being in the moment.

I have found a peace and a calm in my life.

I have found balance in my soul.

And I have learned to open my hands ... and my heart.

I don't know where the road ahead leads. I don't know where my path will take us personally or professionally.

But I know it will be right

I know my life will be full.

And I know ... it already is!

*12.16.16*

## *Epilogue—*

I never meant to take a sabbatical. But that is exactly what I did.

As I read back over each of these passages—I see (and feel) a metamorphosis. I hope as you read it—you experience the changes too. The initial writings in this book feel awkward and disjointed. There are segments that are rough and raw, and others that lack emotion or depth. And yet—the writings themselves are actually part of the story. As the dates progress, the writing becomes clearer. The images sharper. The emotions deeper. It's as if somewhere along the way—the heart found its voice.

This journey begins like a caterpillar—cautiously and slowly looking around the world. Then, as the story transitions—you almost feel like you are tightly wound inside of a cocoon—being nourished, strengthened and yet preparing for something ... Until finally—slowly and beautifully, a butterfly emerges!

I am not the same person I was at the beginning of my *"Accidental Sabbatical."* Professionally and personally—we evolve. We change. We grow. We go through periods of metamorphosis. Sometimes, the changes are subtle. Other times, they are dramatic. And sometimes, they are life-altering—like the butterfly!

In the past two years—a lot has happened in my life. I resigned from a company I loved for many years and thought I would never leave.

I interviewed with several companies. Some I was not right for—and others were not right for me. But in each experience, people came into my life for a reason—either to teach me a lesson about the world—or about myself.

I went back to school and was challenged to my core academically, professionally and personally. I worked with some of the most brilliant minds in the world and wondered often why I was there too. And then I knew …

My mother—my constant friend and rock in my life, was diagnosed with cancer. A disease that changes how you embrace the world and those you love. And in my mother's road to recovery—I developed a rich friendship with my father and learned valuable lessons from my mother. And together—my family found a new strength and bond with one another.

I experienced the first loss of one of our dogs. And in her physical struggles, I saw a strength and passion for life—and learned to be *All Heart* no matter what you are facing.

I discovered a new passion and sport that thrilled me, taught me and brought new people into my life. And in each lesson and session, I learned more about myself than I ever did about the sport.

Our boy Izzy—in his final months of life—relied on me for his health, his strength and his comfort. With him— I learned how to be in the moment. I learned how to hang on ... and how to let go. And I learned no matter what—it will always be okay.

And, I spent almost everyday of the past two years with my husband David. He would challenge me, comfort me, teach me, strengthen me and even make me laugh. I always knew I married a wonderful man. But through him—I could now see the wonderful woman he married.

A lot has happened in the past two years. Some may see this as a dark time in my life. But I see the opposite. I see a time filled with love, learning and rich experiences. A time of discovery and understanding.  A time to become a butterfly

No I never meant to take a sabbatical. But that is exactly what I did.

It was no accident ...

The End ...  and the Beginning!